AF875255

CIMA®

How to access your online resources

Kaplan Financial students will have a MyKaplan account and these extra resources will be available to you online. You do not need to register again, as this process was completed when you enrolled. If you are having problems accessing online materials, please ask your course administrator.

If you are not studying with Kaplan and did not purchase your book via a Kaplan website, to unlock your extra online resources please go to **www.mykaplan.co.uk/add-online-resources** (even if you have set up an account and registered books previously). You will then need to enter the ISBN number (on the title page and back cover) and the unique pass key number contained in the scratch panel below to gain access.

You will also be required to enter additional information during this process to set up or confirm your account details.

If you purchased through the Kaplan Publishing website you will automatically receive an e-mail invitation to register your details and gain access to your content. If you do not receive the e-mail or book content, please contact Kaplan Publishing.

This code can only be used once for the registration of this book online. This registration and your online content will expire when the examinations covered by this book have taken place. Please allow one hour from the time you submit your book details for us to process your request.

Please scratch the film to access your unique code.

Please be aware that this code is case-sensitive and you will need to include the dashes within the passcode, but not when entering the ISBN.

KAPLAN PUBLISHING

CIMA's CGMA® 2019 Professional Examinations

CIMA's CGMA Certificate in Business Accounting

Subject BA2

Fundamentals of Management Accounting

EXAM PRACTICE KIT

CIMA™

KAPLAN PUBLISHING

Published by: Kaplan Publishing UK

Unit 2 The Business Centre, Molly Millars Lane, Wokingham, Berkshire RG41 2QZ

Acknowledgements

We are grateful to the CIMA for permission to reproduce past examination questions. The answers to CIMA Exams have been prepared by Kaplan Publishing, except in the case of the CIMA November 2010 and subsequent CIMA Exam answers where the official CIMA answers have been reproduced. Questions from past live assessments have been included by kind permission of CIMA,

Notice

The text in this material and any others made available by any Kaplan Group company does not amount to advice on a particular matter and should not be taken as such. No reliance should be placed on the content as the basis for any investment or other decision or in connection with any advice given to third parties. Please consult your appropriate professional adviser as necessary.

Kaplan Publishing Limited and all other Kaplan group companies expressly disclaim all liability to any person in respect of any losses or other claims, whether direct, indirect, incidental, consequential or otherwise arising in relation to the use of such materials.

Kaplan is not responsible for the content of external websites. The inclusion of a link to a third party website in this text should not be taken as an endorsement.

Kaplan Publishing's learning materials are designed to help students succeed in their examinations. In certain circumstances, CIMA can make post-exam adjustment to a student's mark or grade to reflect adverse circumstances which may have disadvantaged a student's ability to take an exam or demonstrate their normal level of attainment (see CIMA's Special Consideration policy). However, it should be noted that students will not be eligible for special consideration by CIMA if preparation for or performance in a CIMA exam is affected by any failure by their tuition provider to prepare them properly for the exam for any reason including, but not limited to, staff shortages, building work or a lack of facilities etc.

Similarly, CIMA will not accept applications for special consideration on any of the following grounds:

- failure by a tuition provider to cover the whole syllabus
- failure by the student to cover the whole syllabus, for instance as a result of joining a course part way through
- failure by the student to prepare adequately for the exam, or to use the correct pre-seen material
- errors in the Kaplan Official Study Text, including sample (practice) questions or any other Kaplan content or
- errors in any other study materials (from any other tuition provider or publisher).

British Library Cataloguing in Publication Data

A catalogue record for this book is available from the British Library.

ISBN: 978-1-83735-078-0

Printed and bound in Great Britain

CONTENTS

Section

Quality and accuracy are of the utmost importance to us so if you spot an error in any of our products, please send an email to mykaplanreporting@kaplan.com with full details.

Our Quality Co-ordinator will work with our technical team to verify the error and take action to ensure it is corrected in future editions.

INDEX TO QUESTIONS AND ANSWERS

OBJECTIVE TEST QUESTIONS

EXAM TECHNIQUES

COMPUTER-BASED ASSESSMENT

Golden rules

1 Make sure you have completed the compulsory 15-minute tutorial before you start the test. This tutorial is available through the AICPA & CIMA website and focusses on the functionality of the exam. You cannot speak to the invigilator once you have started.

2 These exam practice kits give you plenty of exam style questions to practise so make sure you use them to fully prepare.

3 Attempt all questions, there is no negative marking.

4 Double check your answer before you put in the final answer although you can change your response as many times as you like.

5 Not all questions will be multiple choice questions (MCQs) – you may have to fill in missing words or figures.

6 Identify the easy questions first and get some points on the board to build up your confidence.

7 Attempt 'wordy' questions first as these may be quicker than the computation style questions. This will relieve some of the time pressure you will be under during the exam.

8 If you don't know the answer, flag the question and attempt it later. In your final review before the end of the exam try a process of elimination.

9 Work out your answer on the whiteboard provided first if it is easier for you. There is also an onscreen 'scratch pad' on which you can make notes. You are not allowed to take pens, pencils, rulers, pencil cases, phones, paper or notes into the testing room.

SYLLABUS GUIDANCE, LEARNING OBJECTIVES AND VERBS

A CIMA's CGMA® 2019 PROFESSIONAL QUALIFICATION

Details regarding the content of CIMA's CGMA 2019 Professional Qualification can be located within the CGMA 2019 Professional Qualification syllabus document.

You can use the following diagram showing the whole structure of your qualification to help you keep track of your progress. Make sure you seek appropriate advice if you are unsure about your progression through the qualification.

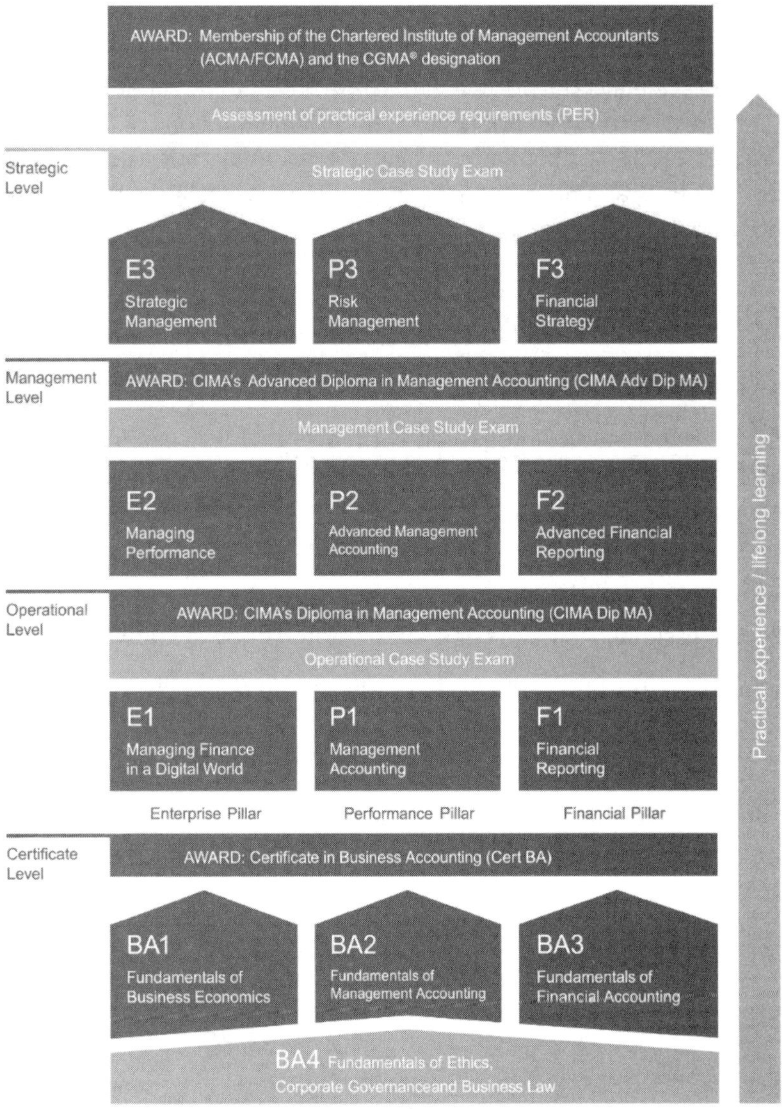

Reproduced with CIMA's permission

B THE CERTIFICATE IN BUSINESS ACCOUNTING (CERTBA)

The CertBA provides a foundation in the essential elements of accounting and business. This includes the Fundamentals of Business Economics. There are four subject areas, which are all tested by computer-based assessment (CBA). The four subjects are:

- BA1: Fundamentals of Business Economics
- BA2: Fundamentals of Management Accounting
- BA3: Fundamentals of Financial Accounting
- BA4: Fundamentals of Ethics, Corporate Governance and Business Law

The CertBA is both a qualification in its own right and an entry route to the next stage in the CGMA examination structure.

The examination structure after the Certificate comprises:

- Operational Level
- Managerial Level
- Strategic Level

The CGMA Professional Qualification includes more advanced topics in Accounting and Business. It is therefore very important that you apply yourself to Fundamentals of Business Economics, not only because it is part of the Certificate in Business Accounting, but also as a platform for more advanced studies. It is thus an important step in becoming a qualified member of the Chartered Institute of Management Accountants.

C AIMS OF THE SYLLABUS

The aims of the syllabus are

- to provide for the Institute, together with the practical experience requirements, an adequate basis for assuring society that those admitted to membership are competent to act as management accountants for entities, whether in manufacturing, commercial or service organisations, in the public or private sectors of the economy;
- to enable the Institute to examine whether prospective members have an adequate knowledge, understanding and mastery of the stated body of knowledge and skills;
- to complement the Institute's practical experience and skills development requirements.

D STUDY WEIGHTINGS

A percentage weighting is shown against each topic in the syllabus. This is intended as a guide to the proportion of study time each topic requires.

All topics in the syllabus must be studied, since any single examination question may examine more than one topic, or carry a higher proportion of marks than the percentage study time suggested.

The weightings do not specify the number of marks that will be allocated to topics in the examination.

E CIMA'S HIERARCHY OF LEARNING OBJECTIVES

CIMA places great importance on the definition of verbs in structuring Objective Test Examinations. It is therefore crucial that you understand the verbs in order to appreciate the depth and breadth of a topic and the level of skill required. The CertBA syllabus learning outcomes and objective test questions will focus on levels one, two and three of the CIMA's hierarchy of learning objectives (knowledge, comprehension and application). However, as you progress to the Operational, Management and Strategic levels of the CGMA Professional Qualification, testing will include levels four and five of the hierarchy. As you complete the CGMA Professional Qualification, you can therefore expect to be tested on knowledge, comprehension, application, analysis and evaluation.

In CertBA Objective Test Examinations you will meet verbs from only levels 1, 2, and 3 of the hierarchy which are as follows:

Skill level	Verbs used	Definition
Level 1 **Knowledge** What you are expected to know	List	Make a list of
	State	Express, fully or clearly, the details/facts of
	Define	Give the exact meaning of
	Outline	Give a summary of

For example you could be asked to define economic terms such as 'inflation' (BA1), or to define the term 'management accounting' (BA2) or to state the accounting entries required to record the revaluation surplus arising on revaluation of land and buildings (BA3).

Skill level	Verbs used	Definition
Level 2 **Comprehension** What you are expected to understand	Describe	Communicate the key features of
	Distinguish	Highlight the differences between
	Explain	Make clear or intelligible/state the meaning or purpose of
	Identify	Recognise, establish or select after consideration
	Illustrate	Use an example to describe or explain something

For example you could be asked to explain the components of the circular flow of funds (BA1), or distinguish between financial accounting and management accounting (BA3) or distinguish between express terms and implied terms of a contract of employment (BA4).

Skill level	Verbs used	Definition
Level 3 Application How you are expected to apply your knowledge	Apply	Put to practical use
	Calculate	Ascertain or reckon mathematically
	Conduct	Organise and carry out
	Demonstrate	Prove with certainty or exhibit by practical means
	Prepare	Make or get ready for use
	Reconcile	Make or prove consistent/compatible

For example you could be asked to reconcile the differences between profits calculated using absorption costing and marginal costing (BA2), or to calculate the gain or loss on disposal of a non-current asset (BA3) or to apply relevant principles to determine the outcome of a law-based or ethical problem (BA4).

For reference, levels 4 and 5 of the hierarchy require demonstration of analysis and evaluation skills respectively. Further detail on levels 4 and 5 of the hierarchy which are tested in the CGMA Professional Qualification can be obtained from the CIMA website, www.cimaglobal.com.

OBJECTIVE TESTS

Objective Test questions require you to choose or provide a response to a question whose correct answer is predetermined.

The most common types of Objective Test question you will see are:

- **multiple choice**, where you have to choose the correct answer(s) from a list of possible answers – this could either be numbers or text.
- **multiple response** with more choices and answers, for example, choosing two correct answers from a list of five available answers – this could either be numbers or text.
- **number entry**, where you give your numeric answer to one or more parts of a question, for example, gross profit is $25,000 and the accrual for heat and light charges is $750.
- **drag and drop**, where you match one or more items with others from the list available, for example, matching several accounting terms with the appropriate definition
- **drop down**, where you choose the correct answer from those available in a drop down menu, for example, choosing the correct calculation of an accounting ratio, or stating whether an individual statement is true or false. This can also be included with a number entry style question.

CIMA has provided the following guidance relating to the format of questions and their marking:

- questions which require narrative responses to be typed will not be used
- for number entry questions, clear guidance will usually be given about the format in which the answer is required e.g. 'to the nearest $' or 'to two decimal places'.
- item set questions provide a scenario which then forms the basis of more than one question (usually 2 and 4 questions). These sets of questions would appear together in the test and are most likely to appear in BA2 and BA3
- all questions are independent so that, where questions are based on a common item set scenario, each question will be distinct and the answer to a later question will not be dependent upon answering an earlier question correctly
- all items are equally weighted and, where a question consists of more than one element, all elements must be answered correctly for the question to be marked correct.

Throughout this Exam Practice Kit we have introduced these types of questions, but obviously we have had to label answers A, B, C etc. rather than using click boxes. For convenience we have retained quite a few questions where an initial scenario leads to a number of sub-questions. There will be questions of this type in the Objective Test Examination but they will rarely have more than three sub-questions.

Guidance on CIMA's on-screen calculator

As part of the CGMA Objective Test software, candidates are now provided with a calculator. This calculator is on-screen and is available for the duration of the assessment. The calculator is available in each of the Objective Tests and is accessed by clicking the calculator button in the top left hand corner of the screen at any time during the assessment. Candidates are permitted to utilise personal calculators as long as they are an approved CIMA model. CIMA approved model list can be found on the AICPA & CIMA website.

All candidates must complete a 15-minute exam tutorial before the assessment begins and will have the opportunity to familiarise themselves with the calculator and practise using it. The exam tutorial is also available online via the AICPA & CIMA website. Candidates can use their own calculators providing it is included in CIMA's authorised calculator listing.

CertBA Objective Tests

The Objective Tests are a two-hour assessment comprising compulsory questions, each with one or more parts. There will be no choice and all questions should be attempted. All elements of a question must be answered correctly for the question to be marked correctly. All questions are equally weighted. The number of questions in each assessment are as follows:

BA1 Fundamentals of Business Economics – 60 questions

BA2 Fundamentals of Management Accounting – 60 questions

BA3 Fundamentals of Financial Accounting – 60 questions

BA4 Fundamentals of Ethics, Corporate Governance and Business Law – 85 questions

CERTBA SYLLABUS GRIDS

BA2: Fundamentals of Management Accounting

Syllabus overview

This subject deals with the fundamental knowledge and techniques that underpin management accounting. It identifies the position of the management accountant within organisations and the role of CIMA. The subject portrays the role of management accounting in the contexts of commercial and public sector bodies and its wider role in society.

The identification and classification of costs and their behaviour provides the basis for understanding and applying the tools and techniques needed to plan, control and make decisions. Budgetary control requires the setting of targets and standards which then allow the performance of organisations to be reported and analysed by the calculation of variances. Investment appraisal, break-even analysis and profit maximisation are used to inform both long and short-term decision making.

Assessment strategy

There will be a two hour computer based assessment, comprising 60 compulsory objective test questions. Short scenarios may be given to which one or more objective test questions relate.

Syllabus structure

The syllabus comprises the following topics and weightings:

Content area		Weighting
A	The context of management accounting	10%
B	Costing	25%
C	Planning and control	30%
D	Decision making	35%
		100%

LEARNING OUTCOMES AND INDICATIVE SYLLABUS CONTENT

BA2A: The context of management accounting (10%)

Learning outcomes

On completion of their studies, students should be able to:

Lead	Component	Level	Indicative syllabus content
1. Explain the purpose of management accounting and the role of the Management Accountant.	a. Explain the need for management accounting. b. Explain the characteristics of financial information for operational, managerial and strategic levels within organisation. c. Explain the role of the management accountant. d. Explain the relationships between the management accountant and the organisation's managers.	2 2 2 2	• The Global Management Accounting Principles. • Characteristics of financial information. • The CIMA definition of the role of the management accountant. • The IFAC definition of the domain of the professional accountant in business. • The positioning of management accounting within the organisation.
2. Explain the role of CIMA as a professional body for Management Accountants.	a. Explain the role of CIMA in developing the practice of management accounting.	2	• The need for a professional body in management accounting. • CIMA's role in relation to its members, students, the profession of management accounting and society.

BA2B: Costing (25%)

Learning outcomes

On completion of their studies, students should be able to:

<table>
<tr><th>Lead</th><th>Component</th><th>Level</th><th>Indicative syllabus content</th></tr>
<tr><td>1. Demonstrate cost identification and classification.</td><td>a. Explain the classification of costs in relation to output.
b. Explain the classification of costs in relation to activity level.
c. Calculate appropriate costs having identified cost behaviour.
d. Explain the classification of costs in relation to decisions.</td><td>2
2
3
2</td><td>• Direct and indirect costs.
• Variable, semi-variable, stepped and fixed costs.
• The use of 'high-low', graphical and regression analysis methods to establish and predict total cost.
• Relevant and irrelevant costs.</td></tr>
<tr><td>2. Apply absorption costing and marginal costing.</td><td>a. Prepare overhead cost statements.
b. Calculate the full cost of products, services and activities.
c. Calculate the marginal cost of products, services and activities.
d. Reconcile the differences between profits calculated using absorption costing and those calculated using marginal costing.
e. Apply cost information in pricing decisions.</td><td>3
3
3
3
3</td><td>• Overhead cost statements: allocation, apportionment and reciprocal servicing.
Note: The repeated distribution and simultaneous equations methods will be used for reciprocal servicing.
• The treatment of direct and indirect costs in ascertaining the full cost of a 'cost object' e.g. a product, service, activity, customer.
• Overhead absorption rates.
• Under or over absorbed overheads.
• The treatment of direct and indirect costs in ascertaining the marginal cost of a 'cost object' e.g. a product, service, activity, customer.
• The difference between marginal and absorption profits.
• Marginal cost pricing and full-cost pricing to achieve specified targets (return on sales, return on investment, mark-up and margins).
Note: Students are not expected to have a detailed knowledge of activity-based costing (ABC).</td></tr>
</table>

BA2C: Planning and control (30%)

Learning outcomes

On completion of their studies, students should be able to:

Lead	Component	Level	Indicative syllabus content
1. Prepare budgets for planning and control.	a. Explain why organisations prepare forecasts and plans b. Prepare functional budgets c. Explain budget statements d. Identify the impact of budgeted cash surpluses and shortfalls on business operations e. Prepare a flexible budget f. Calculate budget variances.	2 3 2 2 3 3	• Budgeting for planning and control. • Functional budgets. • Master budget, including statements of profit and loss, financial position and cash flow. • The importance of cash budgets. • Fixed and flexible budgeting. • Budget variances.
2. Apply variance analysis to reconcile budgeted and actual profits in a marginal format.	a. Explain why planned standard costs, prices and volumes are useful. b. Calculate variances for materials, labour, variable overheads, sales prices and sales volumes. c. Prepare a statement that reconciles budgeted profit with actual profit calculated using marginal costing. d. Explain why variances could have arisen and the inter-relationships between variances.	2 3 3 2	• Principles of standard costing. • Standards for the selling price and variable costs of a product or service. • Variances: materials (total, price and usage); labour (total, rate and efficiency); variable overhead (total, expenditure and efficiency); sales (sales price and sales volume contribution). • The use of variances to reconcile the budgeted and actual profits that have been calculated using marginal costing. • Interpretation of variances.
3. Calculate appropriate financial and non-financial performance measures.	a. Explain the need for appropriate performance measures. b. Calculate appropriate financial and non- financial performance measures in a variety of contexts.	2 3	• Characteristics of service industries. • Responsibility accounting (authority, responsibility and controllability). • The use of appropriate financial and non-financial performance measures in a variety of contexts (e.g. manufacturing and service sectors). **Note:** Detailed knowledge of the balanced scorecard is not required.
4. Prepare accounts and reports for managers.	a. Explain the integration of the cost accounts with the financial accounting system. b. Prepare a set of integrated accounts, showing standard cost variances. c. Prepare appropriate accounts for job and batch costing. d. Prepare reports in a range of organisations.	2 3 3 3	• Manufacturing accounts including raw material, work-in-progress, finished goods and manufacturing overhead control accounts. • Integrated ledgers including accounting for over and under absorption of production overhead. • The treatment of variances in integrated ledger systems. • Job and batch costing. • Cost accounting statements for management information in manufacturing, service and not-for-profit organisations.

BA2D: Decision making (35%)

Learning outcomes

On completion of their studies, students should be able to:

Lead	Component	Level	Indicative syllabus content
1. Demonstrate the impact of risk.	a. Explain the concepts of risk and uncertainty. b. Demonstrate the use of expected values and joint probabilities in decision making. c. Calculate summary measures of central tendency and dispersion for both grouped and ungrouped data. d. Demonstrate the use of the normal distribution.	2 3 3 3	• Risk and uncertainty. • Probability and its relationship with proportions and percentages. • Expected values and expected values tables. • Limitations of expected values. • Arithmetic mean, median, mode, range, variance, standard deviation and coefficient of variation for both ungrouped and grouped data. • Graphs/diagrams and use of normal distribution tables. **Note:** Students will not be asked to apply techniques to deal with uncertainty.
2. Demonstrate the use of appropriate techniques for short-term decision making.	a. Apply breakeven analysis. b. Demonstrate make or buy decisions. c. Calculate the profit maximising sales mix after using limiting factor analysis.	3 3 3	• Breakeven charts, profit volume graphs, breakeven point, target profit, margin of safety. • Make or buy decisions. • Limiting factor analysis for a multi-product company that has one scarce resource.
3. Demonstrate the use of appropriate techniques for long-term decision making.	a. Explain the time value of money. b. Apply financial mathematics. c. Calculate the net present value, internal rate of return and payback for an investment or project.	2 3 3	• The time value of money. • Discounting, compounding, annuities and perpetuities. • Net present value, internal rate of return and payback.

Information concerning formulae and tables will be provided via the CIMA website, www.aicpa-cima.com

Section 1

OBJECTIVE TEST QUESTIONS

THE CONTEXT OF MANAGEMENT ACCOUNTING

1 Which TWO of the following are DISADVANTAGES of Business Process Outsourcing? (place a tick in the box corresponding to any that would apply)

	Higher cost
	Less specialism
	Loss of control
	Duplication of effort
	Confidentiality risk

2 Select the correct word to complete the following sentences.

A The cash budget would be prepared by the management/financial accountant.

B The cash flow statement would be prepared by the management/financial accountant.

C The statement of profit or loss would be prepared by the management/financial accountant.

3 Do the comments below relate to management or financial accounting? Drag each comment under the correct heading.

	Management accounting	**Financial accounting**
Uses only historical data		
Is carried out at the discretion of management		
Uses non-financial information		
Aids planning within the organisation		

4 Which TWO of the following statements regarding information are correct? *(place a tick in the box corresponding to any that would apply)*

☐	Information used by strategic management tends to be summarised
☐	Information used by strategic management tends to be forward looking
☐	Information used by operational management tends to contain estimates
☐	Information used by operational management tends to be required infrequently
☐	Information used by operational management tends to be from external sources

5 Which of the following is NOT a role of management accounting, as defined by CIMA?

A Deriving performance measures and benchmarks for monitoring and controlling

B Measuring and reporting financial and non-financial performance measurements to management and other stakeholders

C Checking the accuracy of the financial statements produced by the organisation

D Formulating strategic and operational plans in line with the corporate objectives of the organisation

6 Management accounting is concerned with planning, control and decision making. Which TWO of the following relate to control? *(place a tick in the box corresponding to any that would apply)*

☐	Preparing an annual budget for a cost centre
☐	Producing an investment appraisal calculation for a proposed new project
☐	Comparing the actual and expected results for a period and calculating the variances
☐	Advising management of the most profitable use of scarce resources
☐	Producing a monthly report of financial and non-financial performance measures for management

7 Which of the following statements regarding information are correct?

A Strategic information is mainly used by middle management in an organisation.

B Productivity measurements are examples of tactical information.

C Operational information is required infrequently by its main users.

D Two characteristics of good information are cost beneficial and regular.

8 Which of the following is NOT one of the five fundamental principles of the CIMA code of ethics?

A Integrity

B Responsibility

C Professional competence and due care

D Confidentiality

9 **Which of the following is a benefit of locating management accounting within the individual business units?**

A Cost saving

B Adoption of best practice

C Closer to the business needs

D Consistency of approach across the organisation

10 **Which of the following is NOT one of the main purposes of management accounting?**

A Planning

B Reporting

C Decision Making

D Controlling

11 **Companies can select different ways to set up their finance function. The three main ways are shown below:**

dedicated business partners	shared services centres	business process outsourcing

Drag and drop the following descriptions to match them with the correct set up.

- The finance staff are an integral part of the business they support.
- The finance function is undertaken by a third party.
- The whole finance function operates as one centre which provides for the finance needs of the whole company.

12 The management accountant of ABC has produced a monthly report for managers. Some of the managers have complained that the report is unhelpful as it misses out some key figures and that they are not always familiar with the terminology used in the report.

Which of the characteristics of good information are missing in this report?

A Accurate and relevant

B Complete and understandable

C Easy to use and accurate

D Understandable and authoritative

13 **Which TWO of the following would normally be carried out by strategic level management?**

- [ ] Making day-to-day decisions about the running of a department
- [ ] Defining the objectives of the company
- [ ] Deciding in which markets to operate
- [ ] Deciding about how to compete within their chosen markets
- [ ] Inventory control

14 **The global management accounting principles help to explain the role of management accounting in today's organisations. The four principles are:**

A Trust, influence, objectivity and reliability

B Integrity, influence, reliability and value

C Honesty, communication, value and relevance

D Trust, influence, value and relevance

15 **Which of the following statements regarding CIMA is INCORRECT?**

A CIMA is committed to upholding the highest ethical and professional standards.

B CIMA can provide students and members with guidance on how to handle situations where their ethics may be compromised.

C CIMA focuses on organisations in the private sector.

D CIMA is the world's largest and leading professional body of management accountants. Members and students are located in over 160 countries.

16 All certified management accountants must comply with CIMA's code of ethics.

A management accountant who puts themselves forward for a role which they do not have the correct knowledge and experience to undertake would be breaching which of the following fundamental principles?

A Integrity

B Objectivity

C Professional competence and due care

D Confidentiality

17 RST operates in the health and fitness industry running a successful chain of fitness centres throughout their home country. A decision has been made to branch out into the fitness clothing industry. A range of clothing will be manufactured for RST which will be sold in their fitness centres.

Select the correct word to complete the sentences regarding levels of decision making.

- The decision on how much inventory of clothing to carry in each fitness centre would be made at the strategic/tactical/operational level.
- The decision to move into the fitness clothing industry would be made at the strategic/tactical/operational level.
- The decision on the range of clothing to sell and the pricing of the range would be made at the strategic/tactical/operational level.

18 Which TWO of the following statements regarding management accounting are correct?

- [ ] Management accounting tends to focus on the needs of external stakeholders.
- [ ] Management accounting information can be presented in any format.
- [ ] The main purpose of management accounting is to produce the statutory financial statements for the entity.
- [ ] Management accounting is carried out at the discretion of management.
- [ ] One of the key deliverables of management accounting is the cash flow statement.

19 Drag the correct word from the following list to complete the sentences regarding the role of the management accountant.

- information
- planning
- enhancing
- control
- reporting
- decision making

The role of the management accountant has changed over the years. Where the role used to be mainly concerned with __________ performance it is now more concerned about __________ performance.

Management accountants are now seen as value-adding business partners. Their main purpose is providing __________ to managers for the purposes of__________, __________ and __________.

20 CIMA's code of ethics is made up of five fundamental principles. Professional competence and due care and professional behaviour are two of the principles. Which THREE of the following make up the five principles?

- [ ] Objectivity
- [ ] Trust
- [ ] Influence
- [ ] Integrity
- [ ] Confidentiality

COSTING

COST IDENTIFICATION AND CLASSIFICATION

21 Select the correct term to complete the following statements:

- Variable
- Fixed
- Stepped
- Semi-variable

_______ costs are conventionally deemed to be constant in total when production volume changes.

With _______ costs the total cost increases in steps as the level of activity increases.

Examples of a _______ cost would be electricity and gas.

_______ costs are conventionally deemed to be constant per unit of output.

22 The total of direct materials, direct labour and direct expenses is known as:

A Production cost

B Contribution

C Prime cost

D Marginal cost

23 In decision making, costs can be deemed to be relevant or irrelevant.

After carrying out some market research, a company is considering manufacturing a new product which will require the purchase of a new machine. To house the new machine, the company will use a part of the factory which is currently rented out to a third party. The third party has been informed that they will no longer be able to rent the space. The production will be able to be carried out by the current staff in the production department.

Consider the following list of costs involved in the decision. Drag the correct term to show if the cost is relevant or irrelevant.

- Relevant
- Irrelevant

The cost of the market research	
The depreciation charge on the new machine	
Rental of factory space	
Labour costs in production department	

24 LMN manufactures one product. The following information about the product is given below:

			$ per unit
Direct materials			10
Direct labour			29
Direct expenses			3
Production overhead	–	variable	7
	–	fixed	5
Non-production costs	–	variable	2
	–	fixed	4
			60

The prime cost per unit is $___________

25 **Direct costs are:**

A costs which can be identified with a cost centre but not identified to a single cost unit

B costs which can be economically identified with a single cost unit

C costs which can be identified with a single cost unit, but it is not economic to do so

D costs incurred as a direct result of a particular decision

26

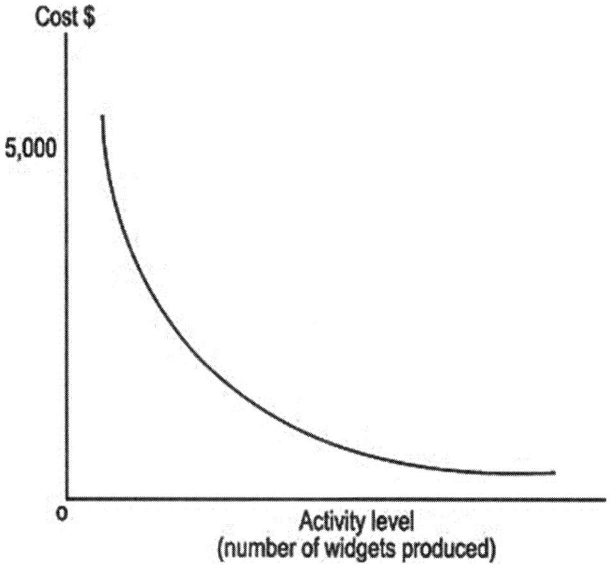

Which of the following descriptions best suits the graph above?

A Total fixed costs

B Total variable costs

C Variable cost per unit

D Fixed cost per unit

27 Which TWO of the following are direct costs?

- ☐ The depreciation of stores equipment
- ☐ The hire of a machine for a specific job
- ☐ Royalty paid for each unit of a product produced
- ☐ Factory rent
- ☐ Factory supervisor's salary

28 Which of the following would be classified as direct labour?

A An HR manager in a company servicing cars

B Builder in a construction company

C General manager in a DIY shop

D Maintenance manager in a company producing cameras

29 Which of the following costs could be being shown in the following diagram?

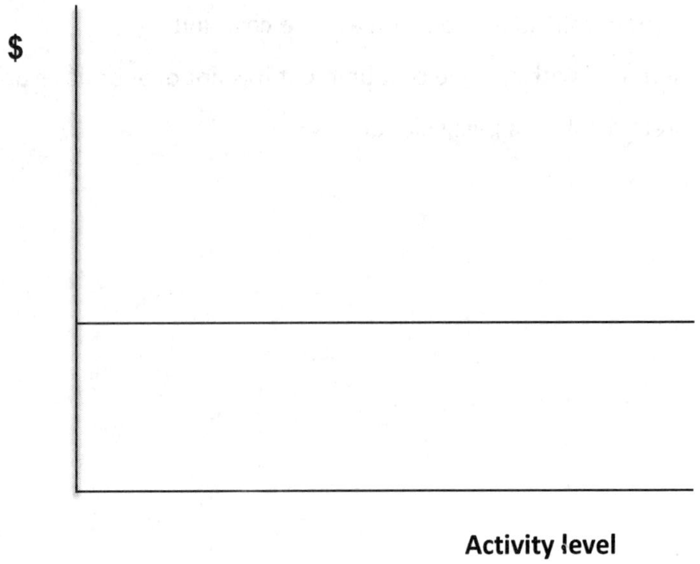

A Total semi-variable costs

B Total variable costs

C Variable cost per unit

D Fixed cost per unit

30 The following is a list of cost units

- Chargeable hour
- Bed-night
- Student
- Batch of 20 pies

Match the most appropriate cost unit to the business to which it is most likely to relate.

A Hotel

B University

C Bakery

D Accounting practice

31 **Match a graph to each of the following costs:**

A Variable cost per unit

B Total fixed cost

C Stepped fixed costs

D Total variable cost

E Total semi-variable cost

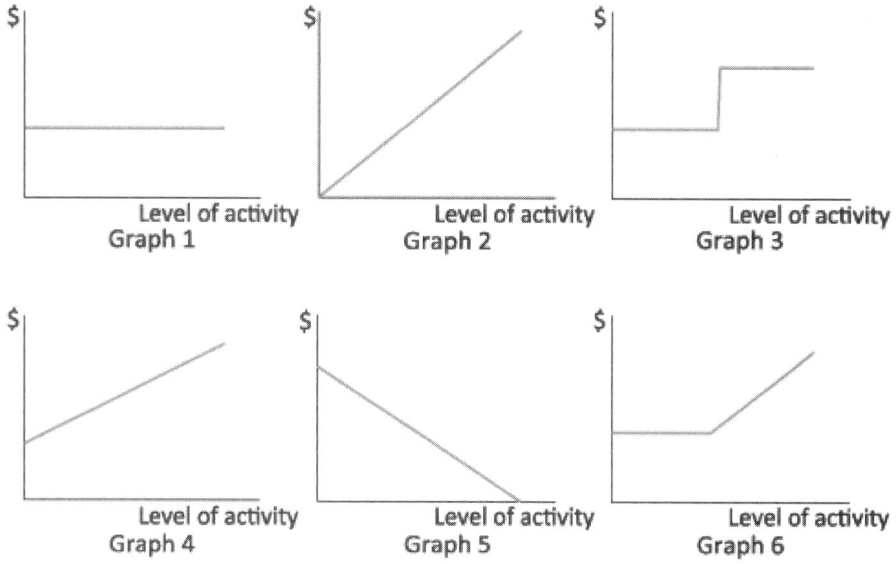

32 **Select the correct word to complete the sentences.**

- The salary of an HR manager in a car servicing company would be classified as direct/indirect labour.
- The salary of a bricklayer in a construction company would be classified as direct/indirect labour.
- The salary of a factory supervisor in a production company would be classified as direct/indirect labour.

33 Over long time periods of several years, supervisory labour costs will tend to behave as which of the following type of cost?

A Linear variable costs

B Stepped fixed costs

C Fixed costs

D Semi-variable costs

34 Select the correct term to complete the following sentences.

- Increase
- Decrease
- Stay the same

As volume decreases, fixed cost per unit will ________ and total fixed costs will ________.

As volume decreases, variable cost per unit will ________ and total variable costs will ________.

35 Select the correct term to complete the following sentences.

A unit of product or service in relation to which costs are ascertained is known as a cost unit/cost centre/cost object.

A production or service location, a function, an activity or an item of equipment for which costs are accumulated is known as a cost unit/cost centre/cost object.

Anything for which costs can be ascertained is known as a cost unit/cost centre/cost object.

ANALYSING AND PREDICTING COSTS

36 The following data have been collected for costs D, E, F and G.

Cost	**Cost for 300 units**	**Cost for 550 units**
	$	$
D	2,100	3,850
E	5,340	6,040
F	3,940	3,940
G	360	660

Tick the relevant box below to indicate the behaviour pattern of each cost.

Cost	**Variable**	**Fixed**	**Semi-variable**
D	☐	☐	☐
E	☐	☐	☐
F	☐	☐	☐
G	☐	☐	☐

37 The following data relate to two output levels of a department:

Machine hours	18,000	20,000
Total overheads	$380,000	$390,000

The variable overhead rate was $5 per machine hour.

The amount of fixed overhead was

A $230,000

B $240,000

C $250,000

D $290,000

38 A company has calculated that the coefficient of determination between output and production costs over a number of months is 89%.

Which TWO of the following comments are correct?

☐	89% of the variation in production costs from one month to the next can be explained by corresponding variation in output.
☐	Costs increase as output increases.
☐	The linear relationship between output and costs is very strong.
☐	An increase of 100% in output is associated with an increase of 89% in costs.
☐	An increase of 89% in output is associated with an increase of 100% in costs.

39 A company has recorded the following information for a six month period.

	Units	**Cost**
July	400	$1,000
August	550	$1,200
September	650	$1,500
October	700	$1,600
November	900	$2,000
December	800	$1,800

Using the high-low method, the total variable cost for September was?

A $200

B $400

C $1,300

D $1,000

40 The following data relate to two output levels of a department:

Units	17,000	18,500
Total cost	$246,500	$251,750

Calculate the variable cost per unit. $___________

41 ABC rents an office photocopier for $300 per month. In addition, the cost incurred per copy taken is $0.02.

If $y = total photocopying cost for the month and x = the number of photocopies taken, which of the following would express the total photocopying cost for a month?

A y = 300 + 2x

B y = 300x + 2

C y = 300 + 0.02x

D y = 300x + 0.02

42 The information below shows the number of calls made and the monthly telephone bill for the first quarter of the latest year:

Month	**No. of calls**	**Cost**
January	800	$2,100
February	1,200	$3,400
March	1,800	$4,600

Using the high–low method the costs could be subdivided into:

A Fixed cost $100 Variable cost per call $2.50

B Fixed cost $100 Variable cost per call $25

C Fixed cost $50 Variable cost per call $2.50

D Fixed cost $50 Variable cost per call $25

43 A travel agency has kept records of the number of holidays booked and the number of complaints received over the past ten years. The data is as follows:

Year	**1**	**2**	**3**	**4**	**5**	**6**	**7**	**8**	**9**	**10**
Holidays booked	246	192	221	385	416	279	343	582	610	674
Complaints	94	80	106	183	225	162	191	252	291	310

The agency suspects there is a relationship between the number of bookings and the volume of complaints and wishes to have some method of estimating the number of complaints, given the volume of bookings.

Using the above the value of the correlation coefficient (r) has been calculated as 0.969.

Which of the following statements is correct?

A 96.9% of the observed changes in the number of complaints can be explained by the changes in the number of holidays booked

B 96.9% of the observed changes in the number of holidays booked can be explained by the changes in the number of complaints

C 93.9% of the observed changes in the number of complaints can be explained by the changes in the number of holidays booked

D 93.9% of the observed changes in the number of holidays booked can be explained by the changes in the number of complaints

44 Consider the following scatter graph.

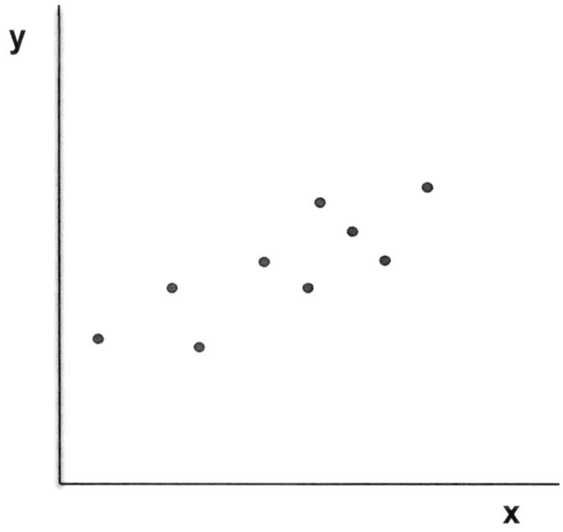

Which of the following correlation coefficients would be most likely for this graph?

A –0.8

B 0

C 0.8

D 1

45 A cleaning company has worked out that the costs incurred in the last 2 months were:

No. of cleaning jobs	Cost
50	$2,235
60	$2,282

The company expects that this pattern of costs will continue. It anticipates that the number of cleaning jobs to be carried out in the next month will be 80.

Calculate the expected total cost if 80 cleaning jobs are undertaken.

OVERHEAD ANALYSIS

46 ABC has completed the initial allocation and apportionment of its overhead costs to cost centres as follows.

Cost centre	Initial allocation
	$000
Machining	190
Finishing	175
Stores	30
Maintenance	25
	420

The stores and maintenance costs must now be reapportioned taking account of the service they provide to each other as follows.

	Machining	Finishing	Stores	Maintenance
Stores to be apportioned	60%	30%	–	10%
Maintenance to be apportioned	75%	20%	5%	

After the apportionment of the service department costs, the total overhead cost of the Finishing department will be (to the nearest $000):

Finishing: $___________

47 A company has produced the following data:

Budgeted machine hours	22,000
Actual machine hours	23,500
Budgeted production overhead	$99,000
Actual production overhead	$111,625

Calculate the machine hour rate for overhead absorption.

A $0.22

B $4.22

C $4.50

D $4.75

48 **Select the correct word to complete the sentences.**

Overhead apportionment/allocation/absorption/reapportionment involves spreading common costs over cost centres on the basis of benefit received.

Overhead apportionment/allocation/absorption/reapportionment involves sharing the costs of service cost centres to production cost centres.

49 A vehicle repair company recovers overhead on the basis of chargeable labour hours.

Budgeted overheads for the latest period were $28,800 and actual chargeable labour hours worked were 400. The actual overheads of $26,700 were over-absorbed by $2,280.

The budgeted overhead absorption rate per chargeable labour hour was $___________ (to 2 decimal places)

50 A company has provided the following data:

Budgeted labour hours	8,500
Budgeted overheads	$148,750
Actual labour hours	7,928
Actual overheads	$146,200

Overheads during the period were:

A Under-absorbed by $2,550

B Over-absorbed by $2,529

C Over-absorbed by $2,550

D Under-absorbed by $7,460

51 **A company absorbs overheads based on machine hours which are budgeted at 11,250 hours at $23 per hour. If actual machine hours worked were 10,980 hours and overheads were $254,692 then overheads were:**

A Under-absorbed by $2,152

B Over-absorbed by $4,058

C Under-absorbed by $4,058

D Over-absorbed by $2,152

52 After the initial overhead allocation and apportionment has been completed, the overhead analysis sheet for a factory is as follows.

Machining	Finishing & packing	Stores	Maintenance	Total
$24,100	$17,930	$5,070	$10,340	$57,440

The cost of maintenance is to be reapportioned to the other three cost centres according to the number of maintenance hours worked, which are as follows.

	Machining	Finishing & packing	Stores
Maintenance hours	3,800	850	50

The maintenance cost (to the nearest $) to be apportioned to the machining department is $___________

53 RST absorbs overheads based on units produced. In one period 110,000 units were produced and the actual overheads were $500,000. Overheads were $50,000 over-absorbed in the period.

The overhead absorption rate was $___________ per unit.

54 In one period the budgeted overheads for a company were $25,000 while the actual overheads were $20,000. Overheads were $2,000 under-absorbed in the period.

Overheads are absorbed on the basis of labour hours. 5,000 labour hours were budgeted for the period.

The actual labour hours in the period were ___________

55 A manufacturing company has two production departments (X and Y) and two service departments (R and S). After primary apportionment the overheads for the factory are as follows:

	Total	X	Y	R	S
Overheads	$633,000	$220,000	$160,000	$140,000	$113,000
Work done by R		45%	35%	–	20%
Work done by S		30%	40%	30%	–

Using the equation method, calculate the total overhead to be apportioned to department X is $___________

56 A company absorbs overheads on labour hours which were budgeted at 11,000. Budgeted overheads were $55,000. Actual hours worked were 10,900 and actual overheads were $57,500.

Which THREE of the following statements are correct?

☐	Overheads were under absorbed
☐	Overheads were over absorbed
☐	The overhead absorption rate was $5.00 per labour hour
☐	The overhead absorption rate was $5.28 per labour hour
☐	The amount of the over/under absorption was $2,500
☐	The amount of the over/under absorption was $3,000

57 A company has four production departments. Overheads have been apportioned between them as follows:

Department	**K**	**L**	**M**	**N**
Overheads	$10,000	$5,000	$4,000	$6,000

The time taken in each department to manufacture the company's only product, X, is 5 hours, 5 hours, 4 hours and 3 hours respectively.

If the company recovers overheads on the basis of labour hours and plans to produce 2,000 units, then the overhead absorption rate per unit is $___________

58 CDE produces two products (X and H) in its factory that is divided into two departments, cutting and stitching. CDE wants to calculate a fixed overhead cost per unit from the following budgeted data. CDE budgets to produce 6,000 units of each product.

	Cutting dept.	**Stitching dept.**
Direct and allocated fixed overheads	$120,000	$72,000
Labour hours per unit		
Product X	0.05 hours	0.20 hours
Product H	0.10 hours	0.25 hours

If fixed overheads are absorbed on the basis of labour hours, the fixed overhead cost of one unit of product H would be $____________

59 Budgeted overheads for a period were $340,000. In the event, actual labour hours and overheads were 21,050 hours and $343,825 respectively.

If there was over-absorption of $14,025, how many labour hours were budgeted?

A 20,000

B 20,225

C 20,816

D 21,050

60 **The management accountant's report shows that fixed production overheads were over absorbed in the last accounting period. Which TWO of the following combination could have led to this situation?**

☐ Production activity higher than budget and actual fixed overhead expenditure as budgeted.

☐ Production activity lower than budget and actual fixed overhead expenditure as budgeted.

☐ Production activity lower than budget and actual fixed overhead expenditure higher than budget.

☐ Production activity as budgeted and actual fixed overhead expenditure more than budget.

☐ Production activity as budgeted and actual fixed overhead expenditure less than budget.

MARGINAL AND ABSORPTION COSTING

61 If the selling price of a product is $150 and the profit margin is 20%, which one of the following statements is true?

A Mark-up is 20%

B Mark-up is 25%

C Mark-up is 33.33%

D Mark-up is impossible to determine without knowing unit cost

62 A company has just completed its first year of trading. The following information has been collected from the accounting records.

Variable production cost per unit	$45.00
Variable selling and administration cost per unit	$20.00
Fixed production costs	$250,000
Fixed selling and administration costs	$25,000

Production and sales were 5,000 units. The selling price was $220 per unit throughout the year.

Calculate the profit using marginal costing.

A $500,000

B $525,000

C $625,000

D $775,000

63 An engineering company is preparing a price for a job. Production overhead is absorbed at the rate of $8.50 per machine hour. In order to allow for non-production overhead costs and profit, a mark-up of 60% of prime cost is added to the production cost.

The following information is available for the job:

Direct materials	$10,650
Direct labour	$3,260
Machine hours	140

Using job costing, the price to be charged for the job is $____________

64 A company plans to produce and sell 5,000 units of product Y in the next period. The unit costs of product Y are given below.

Direct material	$12
Direct labour	$8
Variable production overhead	$5
Fixed production costs	$7
Variable non production costs	$4
Fixed non production costs	$15

Which TWO of the following statements are true?

	The prime cost is $25
	If the selling price was $65, the contribution would be $40
	20% mark-up on total cost would give a selling price of $60
	25% mark-up on total production cost would give a selling price of $40
	15% margin would give a selling price of $60

65 **Which of the following statements is correct, when comparing the profits reported under marginal and absorption costing during a period when the level of inventory decreased?**

A Absorption costing profits will be higher and closing inventory valuations lower than those under marginal costing.

B Absorption costing profits will be higher and closing inventory valuations higher than those under marginal costing.

C Marginal costing profits will be higher and closing inventory valuations lower than those under absorption costing.

D Marginal costing profits will be higher and closing inventory valuations higher than those under absorption costing.

66 Extracts from the budget of ABC for the six months to 31 December are given below:

	$
Sales	55,800
Purchases	38,000
Closing inventory finished goods	7,500
Opening inventory finished goods	5,500

The profit mark-up, as a percentage of the cost of sales (to the nearest whole number) is ____________ %

67 Unit cost information for a product is as follows.

Direct material	$22
Direct labour	$65
Direct labour hours	5 hours

Production overhead is absorbed at a rate of $3 per direct labour hour,

The company requires a 15% profit margin. Mark-up for non-production overhead costs is 8% of total production cost.

Calculate the selling price per unit to the nearest cent. $___________

68 A company has established a marginal costing profit of $72,300. Opening inventory was 300 units and closing inventory is 750 units. The fixed production overhead absorption rate has been calculated as $5 per unit.

What would the profit be under absorption costing?

A $67,050

B $70,050

C $74,550

D $77,550

69 A company is pricing a customer's order. It prices its jobs by adding 20% to the total cost of the job. The prime cost of the job was $6,840 and it had used 156 direct labour hours. The fixed production overheads are absorbed on the basis of direct labour hours. The budgeted overhead absorption rate was based upon a budgeted fixed overhead of $300,000 and total budgeted direct labour hours of 60,000.

What price should be charged for the job?

A $7,620

B $8,208

C $9,144

D $9,525

70 In a period, opening inventory was 12,600 units and closing inventory was 14,100 units.

The profit based on marginal costing was $50,400 and profit using absorption costing was $60,150.

The fixed overhead absorption rate per unit (to the nearest cent) is:

A $4.00

B $4.27

C $4.77

D $6.50

PLANNING AND CONTROL

BUDGETING

The next two questions are based on the following information.

A company manufactures a single product but activity levels vary widely from month to month. The budgeted figures are based on an average activity level of 10,000 units of production.

The actual figures for last month for production of 9,500 units are also shown:

	Budget	Actual
	$	$
Direct labour	10,000	9,400
Materials	5,000	4,800
Variable overhead	5,000	4,300
Depreciation	10,000	10,000
Fixed overhead	5,000	5,200
	35,000	33,700

71 Calculate the variable overhead variance for the month and state if it is adverse or favourable. $____________ adverse/favourable

72 Calculate the fixed overhead variance for the month and state if it is adverse or favourable. $____________ adverse/favourable

73 When preparing a production budget the quantity produced equals which of the following?

A Sales + opening inventory + closing inventory

B Sales + opening inventory – closing inventory

C Sales – opening inventory + closing inventory

D Sales – opening inventory – closing inventory

74 Which of the following best describes budgetary slack?

A Additional time built into the planning process to ensure that all budgets are prepared according to the budget timetable.

B Additional revenue built into the sales budget to motivate the sales team.

C Additional costs built into an expenditure budget to guard against overspending.

D Spare machine capacity that is not budgeted to be utilised.

75 EFG is preparing a cash budget for January. Its credit sales in the last 3 months were:

October	$80,000
November	$60,000
December	$100,000

Estimated credit sales for January are $50,000.

Its recent debt collection experience is

	%
Paid in month of sale	20
Paid one month after sale	60
Paid two months after sale	10
Bad debts	10

A cash discount of 5% is taken for payment in the month of sale

Calculate how much EFG expects to collect in January.

A $70,500

B $75,500

C $76,000

D $80,000

76 A company is analysing its overhead costs for the previous period and has produced the following:

Actual output	162,500 units
Actual overheads	$300,000
Of which: fixed overheads (as budgeted)	$87,000
Adverse variance	$18,000

The company calculates variances based on a flexible budget comparison.

Calculate the budgeted variable cost per unit.

A $0.80

B $1.00

C $1.20

D $1.31

77 A company had a budgeted variable overhead per unit of $2.75. When output was 18,000 units, total overheads were $98,000. Fixed overheads were $11,000 over budget; variable costs were the same as budget.

Calculate the amount budgeted for fixed overheads. $____________

78 A company is preparing its budgets for next year. The following is available for the first three months.

	January	**February**	**March**
Production units	3,500	3,800	3,600
Raw materials (kg):			
Opening inventory	500	800	750
Closing inventory	800	750	600

Each unit requires 2 kg of raw materials. Raw materials cost $4 per kg.

Calculate the raw material usage budget in kg for February. ____________kg

79 There are a number of approaches to budgeting, including:

- Rolling
- Periodic
- Incremental
- Zero-based
- Participative
- Imposed

Match the statements below to the approach to budgeting being discussed.

A With this approach, the budget is prepared by senior managers.

B A disadvantage of this approach is that it can be very time consuming as all budgeted costs must be justified by the expected benefits.

C This approach is more likely to motivate managers as they are involved in the budget preparation

D With this approach the budget is continuously updated.

80 Each unit of product X requires 5 kg of material R. 20% of the input of material R is lost during production. Budgeted production of product X is 1,000 units for the period.

Opening inventory of material R is 200 kg and closing inventory is required to be 100 kg.

What will be the required purchases of material R in the period?

A 3,900 kg

B 4,100 kg

C 6,150 kg

D 6,350 kg

81 **If a company has calculated a volume variance of $7,500 adverse, and an expenditure variance of $3,100 favourable, then the total variance is:**

A $3,100 F

B $4,400 A

C $4,400 F

D $7,500 A

82 The following extract is taken from the maintenance cost budget:

Maintenance hours	8,300	8,520
Maintenance cost	$211,600	$216,440

The budget cost allowance for maintenance costs for the latest period, when 8,427 maintenance hours were worked, is $____________

83 **Use the terms below to complete the sentences on budgeting.**

- Forecast
- Cash budget
- Budget centre
- Budget
- Principal budget factor

The ________ is the limiting factor which determines all other budgets.

A ________ is a section in an organisation for which control may be exercised and budgets prepared.

The objective of a ________ is to anticipate any shortages or surpluses which may arise in the future.

A ________ is a prediction of what is expected to happen, a ________ is a quantified formal plan that the organisation is aiming to achieve.

84 **Select the correct term to complete the sentences.**

A A fixed/flexible budget is designed to change as volume of activity changes.

B Fixed/flexible budgets take no account of production shortfalls.

C Fixed/flexible budgets are useful for control purposes while fixed/flexible budgets are more useful for planning.

STANDARD COSTING AND VARIANCE ANALYSIS

85 **Select the correct word to complete the sentences regarding types of standards.**

1 A standard established for use over a long period of time is known as a(an) ideal/attainable/current/basic standard.

2 A standard which is set taking account of efficiency levels is known as a(an) ideal/attainable/current/basic standard.

3 A standard based on the present performance levels is known as a(an) ideal/attainable/current/basic standard.

4 A standard which makes no allowance for inefficiency is known as a(an) ideal/attainable/current/basic standard.

86 In a given week, a factory has an activity level of 120% with the following output:

	Units	**Standard minutes per unit**
Product A	5,100	6
Product B	2,520	10
Product C	3,150	12

The budgeted direct labour cost was $2,080.

The budgeted standard labour hours were:

A 1,248

B 1,300

C 1,560

D 1,872

87 FGH has calculated the following variances for the latest period:

	$
Sales volume contribution variance	13,420 (F)
Material usage variance	5,400 (F)
Labour rate variance	310 (A)
Variable overhead expenditure variance	6,250 (A)

All other variances were zero. The budgeted contribution for the period was $37,200.

Calculate the actual contribution reported for the period. $____________.

88 **Which TWO of the following statements are INCORRECT?**

- [ ] Both budgets and standards relate to the future
- [ ] Both budgets and standards must be quantified
- [ ] Both budgets and standards are expressed in aggregate terms
- [ ] Both budgets and standards are used in planning
- [ ] Both budgets and standards are expressed in unit terms

89 **If the purchasing manager makes a decision to buy cheaper, inferior raw materials which THREE of the following variances are most likely to result?**

- [ ] favourable material usage
- [ ] adverse material usage
- [ ] favourable labour efficiency
- [ ] adverse labour efficiency
- [ ] favourable material price
- [ ] adverse material price

90 A product has a standard material cost of $32 (4 kg × $8). During May 3,000 kg were purchased at a cost of $23,000. The material usage variance for May was $1,600 adverse and the material price variance was $1,000 favourable. The company holds no inventory.

What was the actual production level for May?

A 700 units

B 750 units

C 800 units

D 850 units

91 A company's materials price variance for January was $1,000 F and the usage variance was $200 F. The standard material usage per unit is 3 kg and the standard material price is $2 per kg. 500 units were produced in the period. Opening inventory of raw materials was 100 kg and closing inventory was 300 kg.

Calculate the material purchases in the period. ___________kg

92 LMN uses a standard costing system. The following details have been extracted from the standard cost card in respect of direct materials:

	Unit cost
Material (8 kg × $0.80/kg)	$6.40

In the last period, budgeted production was 850 units and actual production was 870 units. Material purchased and used in the period was 8,200 kg and cost $6,888.

Which of the following correctly states the material price and usage variances for the period?

A	$286 (A)	$992 (A)
B	$328 (A)	$1,120 (A)
C	$286 (A)	$1,120 (A)
D	$328 (A)	$992 (A)

93 XYZ uses a standard costing system and has the following standard labour cost in relation to its main product:

4 direct labour hours @ $12.00 per hour $48.00

In the last period 3,350 units of this product were made, 150 units less than budget. The labour cost incurred was $159,400 and the number of direct labour hours worked was 13,450.

The direct labour variances for the month were:

	Rate	**Efficiency**
A	$1,400 (A)	$6,600 (F)
B	$1,400 (F)	$600 (A)
C	$2,000 (A)	$6,600 (F)
D	$2,000 (F)	$600 (A)

The next two questions are based on the following information.

The standard selling price of product Y is $34 and the standard variable cost is $20. Budgeted sales volume is 45,000 units per month.

Last month a total of 46,000 units were sold and the revenue achieved was $1,495,000.

94 The sales price variance for the period was $____________

95 The sales volume contribution variance for the period was $____________

96 Which TWO of the following is a possible cause of an adverse labour efficiency variance?

- [ ] The original standard hours were set too high
- [ ] The employees were more skilled than had been planned for
- [ ] Production volume was lower than budget
- [ ] An ideal standard was used for labour time
- [ ] A lower quality of material was used in production

97 Which TWO of the following statements regarding standard costing are correct?

- [ ] Standard costing is a useful technique in dynamic environments.
- [ ] Standard costing is less useful in today's environment because simply achieving standard is no longer seen as acceptable.
- [ ] Standard costing has been criticised as it generally places emphasis on labour variances which is no longer appropriate with the increasing use of automated production techniques
- [ ] Standard costing is only really useful in manufacturing environments.
- [ ] Standard costing encourages companies to strive for continuous improvement.

98 Insert some of the following words to complete the sentences below regarding standard costing. Not all words need to be used and words can be used more than once.

- Actual
- Budgeted
- Standard
- Higher
- Lower

The direct labour rate variance is calculated by comparing the _______ labour cost with the _______ labour rate flexed by the ________ number of hours worked.

An adverse direct labour rate variance suggests that the actual labour cost was ______than expected.

INTEGRATED ACCOUNTING SYSTEMS

99 In an integrated accounting system, the accounting entries for production overhead absorbed would be:

A Debit WIP control account
Credit overhead control account

B Debit overhead control account
Credit WIP account

C Debit overhead control account
Credit cost of sales account

D Debit cost of sales account
Credit overhead control accounts

100 RST operates a standard integrated accounting system. In a period the actual material usage has been greater than the standard material usage.

Tick the correct accounting entries below to show how this would be recorded.

	Debit	**Credit**	**No entry in this account**
Material usage variance account			
Raw material control account			
Work-in-progress account			

101 **A company uses standard costing and an integrated accounting system. The accounting entries for a favourable labour efficiency variance are:**

	Debit	**Credit**
A	WIP control account	labour efficiency variance account
B	labour efficiency variance account	WIP control account
C	wages control account	labour efficiency variance account
D	labour efficiency variance account	wages control account

The next two questions are based on the following information.

The following analysis of labour costs for a department has been produced. Direct employees are directly involved in production while indirect employees are involved indirectly with production, or in support functions.

	Direct Employees	**Indirect employees**
Basic pay	55,000	22,750
Overtime – basic rate	2,400	
Overtime premium	600	
Bonuses	1,000	1,500
	59,000	27,750

102 Use the costs from the above table to complete the analysis of direct and indirect labour costs.

	Direct labour costs	**Indirect labour costs**
Basic pay – direct employees		
Basic pay – indirect employees		
Overtime – basic rate		
Overtime premium		
Bonuses – direct employees		
Bonuses – indirect employees		

103 Complete the following sentences by selecting the correct word.

1 If the overtime worked by direct employees was to complete a specific job for a customer, overtime premium would be treated as direct/indirect costs.

2 If the bonuses were paid for completion of a particular task, the bonuses would be treated as direct/indirect costs.

104 At the end of a period a company using an integrated accounting system calculated that they had an adverse labour rate variance.

Which TWO of the following entries would be required to record this?

- [ ] CR Work in progress account
- [ ] DR Work in progress account
- [ ] DR Labour rate variance account
- [ ] CR Labour rate variance account
- [ ] CR Wages control account
- [ ] DR Wages control account

105 Which TWO of the following statements relating to integrated accounting are true?

	If a company operates an integrated accounting system, they need to undertake a periodic reconciliation to ensure the cost and financial ledgers agree
	Control accounts are used as summary accounts to record the total entries for each ledger.
	Integrated accounting systems may not provide the quality of information required for management accounting purposes.
	Maintaining integrated accounting systems can result in duplication of work.
	With an integrated accounting system different profit figures can be calculated for financial and management accounting purposes.

106 When materials are purchased on credit, what would be the relevant integrated accounting entry?

A Debit Work-in progress account
Credit Material control account

B Debit Material control account
Credit Accounts payable account

C Debit Material control account
Credit Work-in progress account

D Debit Cost of sales account
Credit Material control account

107 Consider the following entries taken from the WIP control account:

1	Wages	\$30,000
2	Production overhead	\$40,000
3	Transfer to finished goods	\$350,000
4	Balance carried forward	\$75,000

Calculate the value of raw materials brought into production. \$___________

PERFORMANCE MEASUREMENT

108 Drag the correct word from the list below to complete the table about the performance measures used in responsibility accounting.

- Cost centre
- Profit centre
- Investment centre

Department	Performance measure	Type of centre
A	ROCE	
B	Total costs	
C	Gross profit %	

109 Which TWO of the following statements regarding the balanced scorecard are correct?

☐	The learning and growth perspective focuses on the need for continual improvement of existing products and techniques
☐	The goal of reducing staff turnover would be used in the learning and growth perspective
☐	The balanced scorecard uses only non-financial performance measures
☐	The goal of increasing return on capital employed would be used in the financial perspective
☐	The four perspectives in the balance scorecard are customer, internal effectiveness, profit and learning and growth

---

The next two questions relate to the following data.

XYZ runs a chain of fitness centres. It uses a balanced scorecard approach and has set the following goals for the period.

- To reduce the number of customer complaints
- To increase the number of new members
- To reduce the cost per member

The following data have been provided:

	Year 1	**Year 2**
Total members	8,800	9,100
of which – new	1,300	700
of which – existing	7,600	8,400
Complaints	560	565
Total cost	$14.08m	$14.287m

---

110 Which TWO of the following statements regarding XYZ's performance are true?

☐	XYZ has failed to succeed in meeting any of its goals
☐	XYZ's cost per member in Year 1 was $1,600
☐	XYZ's number of complaints per member in Year 2 was 0.062
☐	XYZ's total cost has increased by 3.4%
☐	XYZ's number of total members has increased by 1.47%

111 Select the correct term to complete the following sentences:

A XYZ's number of complaints has increased/decreased and its number of complaints per member has increased/decreased.

B XYZ's total cost has increased/decreased and its total cost per member has increased/decreased.

C XYZ's number of new members has increased/decreased and its number of repeat members has increased/decreased.

---

112 Which of the following is NOT an example of a composite cost unit?

A Kilowatt hours

B Meals served

C Patient days

D Tonne miles

113 Which of the following would be the most appropriate cost unit for a distribution company?

A Miles travelled

B Tonnes carried

C Tonne miles

D Packages delivered per driver

114 R is the manager of production department M in a factory which has ten other production departments. After department M, all production goes into other factory departments to be completed prior to being despatched to customers.

R receives monthly information that compares planned and actual expenditure for department M. Decisions involving capital expenditure in department M are not taken by R.

Which of the following describes R's role in department M?

A A cost centre manager

B An investment centre manager

C A profit centre manager

D A revenue centre manager

115 Insert some of the following terms to complete the balanced scorecard diagram.

Vision and strategy	Financial	Supplier	Profit
Learning and growth	Productivity	Internal business processes	Customer

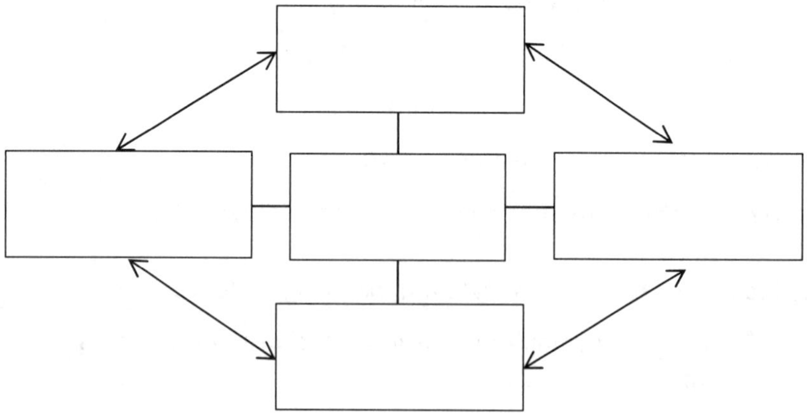

The next two questions relate to the following data:

Companies CDE and PQR operate in the same industry. Data for both companies for the last financial year are given.

	CDE	**PQR**
	$000	$000
Sales revenue	8,800	9,100
Operating profit	1,300	700
Capital employed	7,600	8,400

116 Calculate the ROCE for both companies. (to 1 decimal place)

CDE ____________%

PQR ____________%

117 Calculate the operating margin % for both companies. (to 1 decimal place)

CDE ____________%

PQR ____________%

PREPARING ACCOUNTS AND REPORTS FOR MANAGEMENT

The next two questions relate to the following data.

A company uses job costing and recovers overheads on the basis of direct labour cost.

Three jobs were worked on during a period, the details of which were

	Job 1	**Job 2**	**Job 3**
	$	$	$
Opening work-in-progress	8,500	0	20,000
Material in period	17,150	29,025	5,000
Labour for period	12,500	23,000	4,500

The overheads for the period were $140,000, exactly as budgeted. Jobs 1 and 2 were incomplete at the end of the period.

118 What was the value of closing work-in-progress?

A $81,900

B $90,175

C $140,675

D $214,425

119 Job 3 was completed during the period and consisted of 1,500 identical components. The company adds 25% to total production costs to arrive at a selling price.

What is the selling price of a component?

A $21.04

B $24.58

C $37.71

D $40.22

120 **A retailer buys in a product for $50 per unit and wishes to achieve a gross profit % of 40%. The selling price should be:**

A $70.00

B $83.33

C $90.00

D $125.00

The next two questions are based on the following data.

A small management consultancy has prepared the following information:

Overhead absorption rate per consulting hour	$12.50
Salary cost per consulting hour (senior)	$20.00
Salary cost per consulting hour (junior)	$15.00

The company adds 40% to total cost to arrive at a selling price.

Job number 652 took 86 hours of a senior consultant's time and 220 hours of a junior consultant's time.

121 **What price should be charged for job 652?**

A $5,355

B $7,028

C $8,845

D $12,383

122 During a period 3,000 consulting hours were charged out in the ratio of 1 senior to 3 junior hours. Overheads were exactly as budgeted.

Calculate the gross profit for the period. $____________

123 **The total estimated cost of a job $2,080. The company requires a profit margin of 20%. The price to be quoted for the job is $____________**

The next two questions are based on the following data:

PQR specialises in printing high quality business cards. The most popular requirement is for a coloured business card printed on both sides. From past records and budgeted figures, the following data have been estimated for a typical batch of 100 cards:

Artwork	$40
Machine setting	3 hours @ $15 per hour
Card	$2 per A4 sheet (each A4 sheet will produce 10 business cards)
Ink and consumables	$10
Printers' wages	1 hour @ $10 per hour

Note: Printers' wages vary with volume.

PQR adds 20% to direct costs to cover overheads.

PQR wishes to achieve a 30% profit margin.

124 The direct cost of producing 100 business cards is:

A $85

B $107

C $115

D $125

125 Calculate the price to be quoted for a batch of 200 cards. $________. (to the nearest $)

126 Service industries have four main features:

- Intangibility
- Perishability
- Variability
- Inseparability

Insert the terms against the correct definition.

Each service is unique and cannot usually be repeated in the same way.	
Services cannot be stored for use at a later date.	
Services generally have simultaneous production and consumption.	
Services often have few, if any, physical attributes.	

The next two questions are based on the following information.

A transport company has three divisions and you are given the following data.

	Division A	Division B	Division C
Sales ($000)	200	300	250
No. of vehicles	50	20	10
Distance ('000 km)	150	100	50
Identifiable fixed costs	25	30	35

Variable costs are $300,000 for the company as a whole and are estimated to be incurred in the ratio of 1:4:5 respectively for A, B and C.

The fixed costs which are not directly identifiable are $75,000. These are shared equally between the three divisions

127 Calculate the contribution of division A. $__________

128 Calculate the contribution per kilometre of division B. $__________

129 Select the correct term to complete the following sentences:

- If a hospital compared the current waiting time for patients against the target time, this would be a measure of economy/efficiency/effectiveness.
- If a school compared the % passes for actual exam results compared to target exam results, this would be a measure of economy/efficiency/effectiveness.
- If a university measured the % of graduates who found full time employment within a year of graduating, this would be a measure of economy/efficiency/effectiveness.

130 Which TWO of the following are contained in a typical job cost sheet?

☐	Actual material cost
☐	Actual manufacturing overheads
☐	Absorbed manufacturing overheads
☐	Budgeted labour cost
☐	Budgeted material cost

DECISION MAKING

RISK – SUMMARISING AND ANALYSING DATA

131 XYZ provides catering at football matches. It is analysing the number of games worked by their members of staff over the last 40 games. The following frequency distribution has been produced.

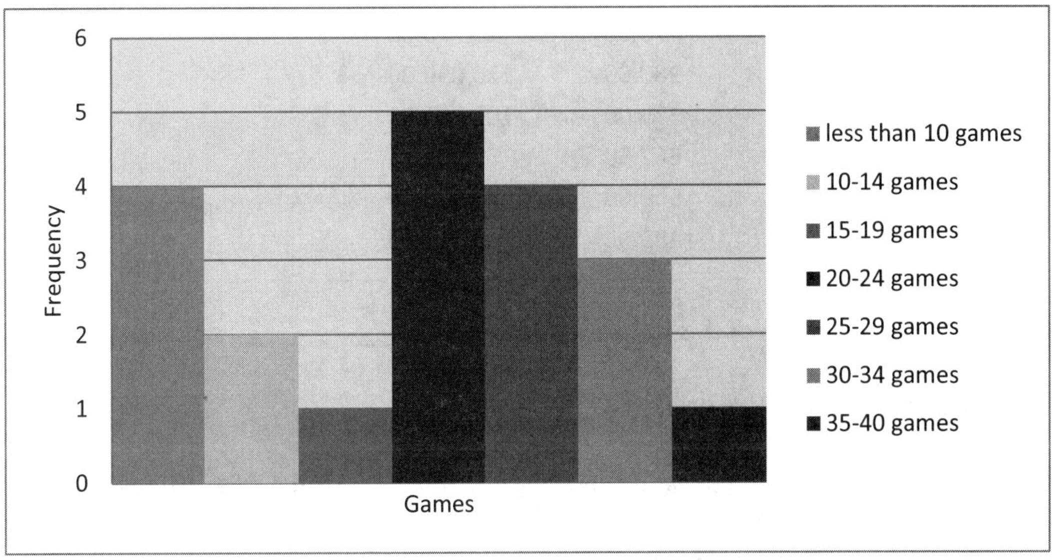

Using the data given in the frequency distribution, which TWO of the following statements are correct?

- ☐ 8 members of staff worked less than 20 games
- ☐ XYZ have 20 members of staff in total
- ☐ 4 members of staff worked 30 or more games
- ☐ The most popular number of games to have worked is 25 – 29
- ☐ Only 4 members of staff could have worked all 40 games

132 A farmer has land extending to 100 acres which comprises 43% wheat, 20% barley, 16% grass, 12% oats and 9% fallow.

If these figures were drawn in a pie chart, calculate the angle of the following crops (To the nearest whole number):

- Wheat ____________
- Oats ____________

The next two questions use the following data:

Some details from a frequency distribution of time taken in seconds to produce a particular product are given:

Time taken (mid-point)	f	fx	fx^2
107.5	2	215.00	23,112.50
112.5	5	562.50	63,281.25
117.5	4	470.00	55,225.00
122.5	8	980.00	120,050.00
127.5	10	1,275.00	162,562.50
132.5	5	662.50	87,781.25
137.5	4	550.00	75,625.00
142.5	2	285.00	40,612.50

133 Calculate the mean of this frequency distribution. ____________ seconds

134 Calculate the standard deviation. ____________

135 Consider the following diagram showing a company's annual sales figures in a number of countries over two years..

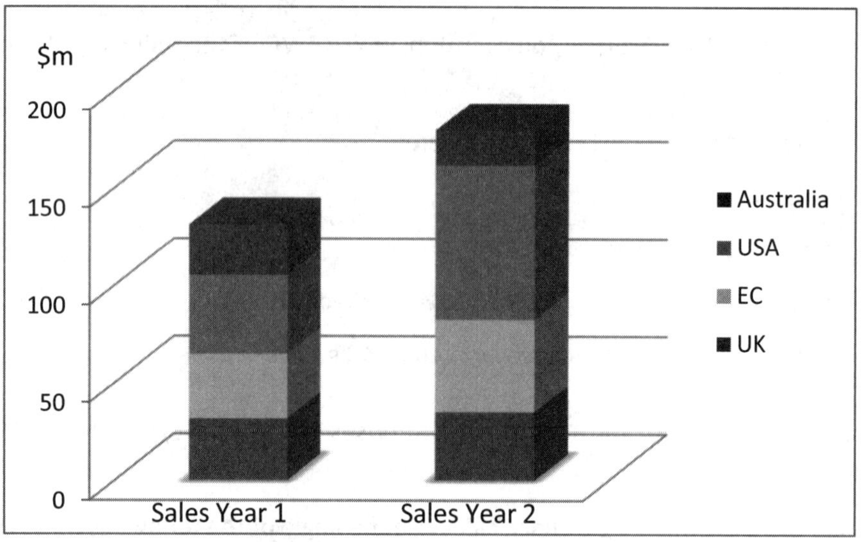

What type of chart is shown here?

A Simple bar chart

B Pie chart

C Histogram

D Component bar chart

136 A histogram uses a set of rectangles to represent a grouped frequency table. To be correctly presented, the histogram must show the relationship of the rectangles to the frequencies by reference to the

A height of each rectangle

B area of each rectangle

C width of each rectangle

D diagonal of each rectangle

137 In a pie chart, if wages are represented by 90° and the total cost is $550,000, what is the amount paid out in wages?

A $135,000

B $137,500

C $142,000

D $145,000

138 In a histogram cumulative frequencies are plotted against:

A the mid-point

B the lower class boundaries

C the upper class boundaries

D any of the above

139 The mean weight of 10 parcels is 20 kg. The individual weights in kilograms are:

15, x, 22, 14, 21, 15, 20, x, 18 and 27.

Calculate the value of x. ____________ kg

140 Select the correct word to complete the sentences.

- The mean/median/mode is the value which appears with the highest frequency
- The mean/median/mode is calculated by adding all of the values and dividing the total by the number of values
- The mean/median/mode is the middle of a set of values

141 The following shows the number of orders placed by customers in the last period.

Number of orders	Frequency
1	3
2	5
3	12
4	14
5	6

Calculate the standard deviation. ____________

The next THREE questions are based on the following data:

A sample of 12 packets of crisps taken from a box had the following weights in grams:

504, 506, 501, 505, 507, 506, 504, 508, 503, 505, 502, 504.

142 Calculate the mean weight.

A 502.3

B 503.4

C 504.6

D 505.7

143 Calculate the median weight.

A 504.0

B 504.5

C 505.0

D 505.5

144 Calculate the modal weight.

A 504

B 505

C 506

D 507

145 CDE runs a race track. The following numbers in seconds show the lap times of 40 drivers.

126	120	122	105	129	119	131	138	130	112
123	127	113	112	130	122	134	136	142	106
128	126	117	114	120	123	127	140	135	122
124	127	114	111	116	131	128	137	116	127

CDE wishes to group the data into eight classes. The analysis has been started below but some figures are missing.

Drag some of the following numbers to complete the frequency distribution.

6 10 125 9 150 5 140

Time		Frequency
105 >	110	2
110 >	115	[ ]
115 >	120	4
120 >	[ ]	8
125 >	130	[ ]
130 >	135	5
135 >	[ ]	4
140 >	145	2

146 Consider the three averaging methods:

- Mean
- Median
- Mode

Match the following disadvantages with the method to which it relates:

A Data has to be arranged in order of size which is time consuming

B It may give undue weight or be influenced by extreme values

C Data has to be arranged to ascertain which figure appears the most often

RISK – PROBABILITY

147 A company is deciding whether to order 100, 200 or 300 units in the next period. The following payoff table has been completed to show the profit in $000 for each potential outcome.

		Order		
Demand	**Probability**	100	200	300
100	0.25	10	(20)	(60)
200	0.40	10	30	0
300	0.35	10	30	80

In order to maximise expected profit, how many units should the company order?

____________ **units**

148 **Which TWO of the following are NOT features of a normal distribution?**

- [ ] It is symmetrical
- [ ] It is bell-shaped
- [ ] The area under the curve is equal to 0.5
- [ ] The mean is equal to the mode
- [ ] The mean is above the median

149 ABC is a supermarket. The manager is deciding how many boxes of fresh fish to purchase for the next day. Each box costs $10 and sells for $30, but any unused inventory at the end of the day will be disposed of.

A review of sales from the last few months has revealed that demand is likely to be either 4, 5 or 6 boxes.

The following payoff table has been produced although there are a few items missing.

	Order		
Demand	**4 boxes**	**5 boxes**	**6 boxes**
4 boxes	80	70	
5 boxes	80	100	
6 boxes	80		

Calculate the missing entries to complete the payoff table.

150 Fill in the missing words from the following list to complete the sentences.

- exact
- empirical
- subjective

A When a situation can be repeated a number of times this is classed as __________ probability.

B Where estimates are made by individuals of the relative likelihood of events occurring, this is called __________ probability.

C When the probability can be applied to the population of outcomes this is called __________ probability.

151 If the three possible outcomes of a decision are profits of $10, $50 or $80 with probabilities of 0.3, 0.3 and 0.4 respectively, what is the expected profit?

A $40

B $44

C $47

D $50

152 A local council is considering purchasing a snow plough which would cost $20,000 per annum. This would save on outside contractors but the amount would depend on the severity of the winter weather.

Weather	**Annual savings**	**Probability**
severe	$40,000	0.2
average	$20,000	0.5
mild	$10,000	0.3

Based on the above figures, calculate the cost or saving for the council if they bought their own plough. $__________ saving/cost

153 A new product is expected to generate the following profits or losses:

Level of demand	**Profit/Loss**	**Probability**
high	$100,000	0.1
medium	$50,000	0.5
low	$20,000 loss	0.4

Calculate the expected profit or loss from the new product. $__________

154 **A company is deciding between three projects A, B and C. The expected profit from each one is as follows:**

Project A		Project B		Project C	
Profit	**Probability**	**Profit**	**Probability**	**Profit**	**Probability**
$5,000	0.5	$10,000	0.3	$6,000	0.4
$2,500	0.5	$1,000	0.7	$4,000	0.6

Rank projects in descending order by inserting 1 beside the highest ranked project, 2 beside the second and 3 beside the third.

	Rank
Project A	
Project B	
Project C	

155 An organisation has surveyed its customers. 35% of its customers responded of which only 54% said that they would recommend the organisation to others.

Based on expected value principles, calculate the percentage of customers overall that are likely to recommend the organisation to others. ____________ %

156 In a room there are 100 CGMA candidates. Twenty per cent identify as being non-binary. Sixty per cent of all the candidates have passed CertBA and 40% have yet to do so.

Calculate the probability of selecting at random a person who is non-binary and has passed CertBA. ____________ %

157 Twenty-five per cent of new cars of a particular model are supplied from factory X. The remainder come from factory Y. Ten per cent of factory X's output has a major fault whilst 18% of factory Y's output has the same fault.

Calculate the probability that a car selected at random has a major defect____________ %

158 XYZ currently earns profit of $500,000. It is considering making a new investment which could increase or decrease profit and has produced the following decision tree to help make the decision.

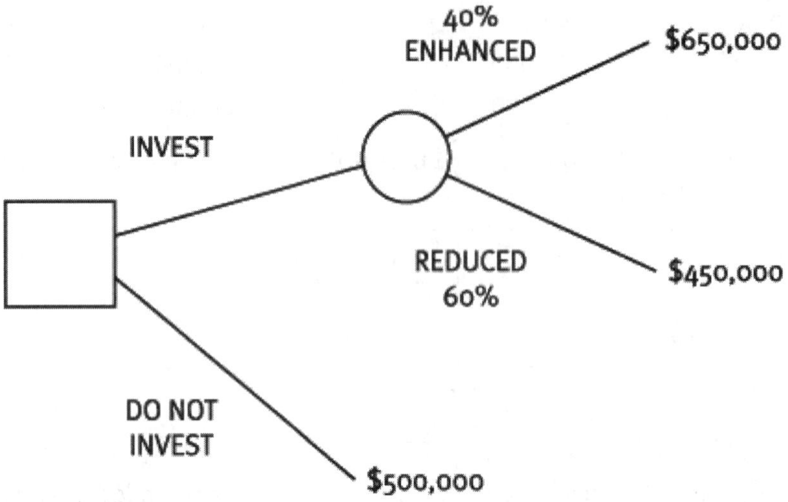

Which of the following statements regarding the decision tree is correct?

A XYZ would be willing to pay up to $30,000 for the investment

B XYZ would be willing to pay up to $50,000 for the investment

C XYZ would be willing to pay up to $150,000 for the investment

D The investment is not worth doing

The next TWO questions are based on the following data:

A group of workers have a weekly wage which is normally distributed with a mean of $360 per week and a standard deviation of $15.

---

159 What is the probability that a worker earns less than $330?

A 1.3%

B 2.3%

C 3.1%

D 4.6%

160 What is the probability that a worker earns between $370 and $400?

A 1%

B 15%

C 20%

D 25%

SHORT-TERM DECISION MAKING

161 Product X generates a contribution to sales ratio of 50%. Fixed costs directly attributable to product X are $100,000 per annum.

Calculate the sales revenue required to achieve an annual profit of $125,000.

$ ___________

162 ABC wishes to draw a basic break-even chart for its only product. Which of the following information would NOT be required?

A Selling price

B Variable cost per unit

C Fixed cost

D Margin of safety

163 A company makes a single product which it sells for $10 per unit. Fixed costs are $48,000 and the contribution to sales ratio is 40%.

If projected sales are $140,000, what is the margin of safety in units?

A 2,000

B 3,000

C 4,000

D 5,000

164

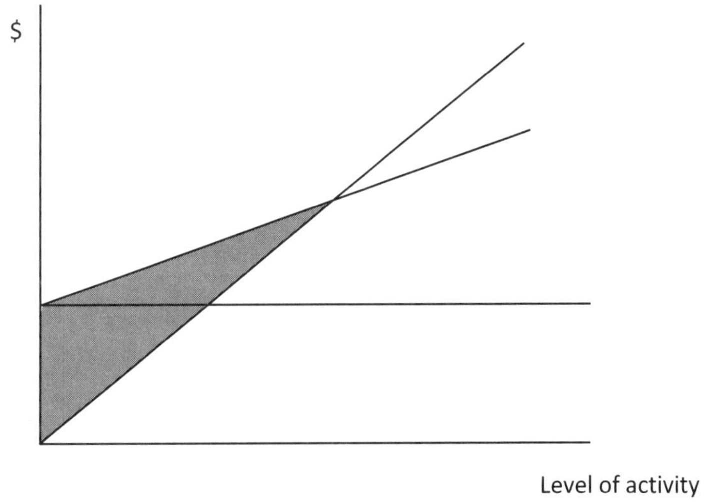

The shaded area on the breakeven chart above represents:

A loss

B fixed cost

C variable cost

D profit

165 Which TWO of the following statements are correct?

☐	The point where the total cost line cuts the vertical axis is the breakeven point on a traditional breakeven chart.
☐	The point where the total cost line cuts the horizontal axis is the breakeven point on a traditional breakeven chart.
☐	The point where the profit line cuts the horizontal axis is the breakeven point on a profit-volume chart.
☐	The point where the profit line cuts the vertical axis is the breakeven point on a profit-volume chart.
☐	The point where the total cost line and the total sales revenue line intersect is the breakeven point on a traditional breakeven chart.

166 Product R sells for $45 per unit and incurs variable costs of $15 per unit and fixed costs of $30,000.

The line drawn on a profit-volume chart will cut the vertical (*y*) axis at the point where *y* = ____________

The next two questions are based on the following information.

A product has produced the following statement which relates to sales of 1,000 units:

	$
Sales	15,000
Variable Costs	9,000
Fixed Costs	4,500

167 The contribution to sales ratio is:

A 25%

B 60%

C 40%

D Impossible to determine

168 The margin of safety is:

A 15%

B 25%

C 40%

D 50%

The next two questions are based on the following data.

A company makes a single product and budgets to produce and sell 7,200 units each period. Cost and revenue data for the product at this level of activity are as follows.

	$ per unit
Selling price	53
Direct material cost	24
Direct labour cost	8
Other variable cost	3
Fixed cost	7
Profit	11

169 The contribution to sales ratio (C/S ratio) is ___________% (to the nearest whole number).

170 The margin of safety % is ___________%. (to the nearest whole number)

171 X is currently employed by ABC. She is contemplating leaving her job and starting her own business.

In considering whether or not to start her own business, which of the following would be the best description of X's current salary?

A a sunk cost

B an incremental cost

C an irrelevant cost

D an opportunity cost

172 P is considering accepting a contract. The materials required for the contract are currently held in inventory at a book value of $3,000. The materials are not regularly used by the organisation and currently have a scrap value of $500. Current replacement cost for the materials is $4,500.

The relevant cost to P of using the materials on this contract is $___________

173 ABC makes a single product which requires $5 of materials, 2 hours of labour and 1 hour of machine time.

Each week there is $500 available for materials, 80 hours of labour and 148 hours of machine time. The limiting factor is?

A Materials

B Labour

C Machine time

D All of the above

174 In order to complete a special order, a company needs two materials, S and T. Material S is commonly used within the business whereas material T is no longer used.

Information for the two materials:

	Required for order	**In Inventory**	**Original cost**	**Replacement cost**	**Net realisable value**
	kg	kg	$/kg	$/kg	$/kg
Material S	2	15	2.40	4.20	1.80
Material T	3	20	1.00	1.40	0.40

Which TWO of the following statements are true?

☐	The relevant cost of S is $4.80
☐	The relevant cost of S is $8.40
☐	The relevant cost of S is $3.60
☐	The relevant cost of T is $3.00
☐	The relevant cost of T is $4.20
☐	The relevant cost of T is $1.20

175 A company makes three products as follows:

	A	**B**	**C**
	$	$	$
Material at $5 per kg	5.00	2.50	10.00
Labour at $12 per hour	36.00	12.00	12.00
Fixed costs absorbed	6.00	2.00	2.00
Profit	6.00	3.50	5.00
Selling price	53.00	20.00	29.00

Maximum demand is 1,000 of each product. In a period labour is limited to 1,000 hours. To maximise profits the company should produce:

A 1,000 of A

B 1,000 of B

C 1,000 of C

D 333 of each product

176 For the forthcoming year, variable costs are budgeted to be 60% of sales value and fixed costs to be 10% of sales value. If the selling price increases by 10% and fixed costs, variable costs per unit and sales volume remain the same, the effect on contribution would be?

A A decrease of 5%

B No change

C An increase of 15%

D An increase of 25%

177 XYZ manufactures three products, the selling price and cost details of which are given below:

	Product X	**Product Y**	**Product Z**
	$	$	$
Selling price per unit	79	101	95
Costs per unit:			
Direct materials ($5/kg)	10	5	15
Direct labour ($10/hour)	20	30	20
Variable overhead	8	12	10
Fixed overhead	24	36	30

In a period when direct materials are restricted in supply, the most and the least profitable uses of direct materials are:

	Most profitable	**Least profitable**
A	X	Z
B	Y	Z
C	X	Y
D	Z	Y

178 RST is currently experiencing a shortage of skilled labour. In the coming quarter only 3,600 hours will be available for the production of its three products, for which details are shown below:

Product	**X**	**Y**	**Z**
Selling price per unit	$66	$100	$120
Variable cost per unit	$42	$75	$90
Fixed cost per unit	$30	$34	$40
Skilled labour per unit	0.40 hours	0.50 hours	0.75 hours
Maximum quarterly demand	5,000	5,000	2,000

Select the correct number to complete the sentences showing the optimum production plan that will maximise profit for the quarter.

- To maximise profit, RST should produce 0/3,200/5,000 units of X
- To maximise profit, RST should produce 0/3,200/5,000 units of Y
- To maximise profit, RST should produce 0/3,200/5,000 units of Z

179 A company, which manufactures four components (A, B, C and D) using the same machinery, aims to maximise profit. The following information is available:

	Component			
	A	**B**	**C**	**D**
Variable production cost per unit ($)	60	64	70	68
Machine hours per unit	4	7	5	6
External purchase price per unit ($)	100	120	130	110

As it has insufficient machine hours available to manufacture all the components required, the company will need to buy some units of one component from the outside supplier.

Which component should be purchased from the outside supplier?

A Component A

B Component B

C Component C

D Component D

180 **ABC manufactures a range of products. It is considering outsourcing the manufacture of one of its products, the M2. Budgeted details for the M2 are as follows:**

	$
Selling price	8.00
Costs per unit:	
Direct materials	3.00
Direct labour	1.00
Variable overhead	0.40
Fixed overhead	1.00
Profit per unit	2.60

Budgeted production and sales for the year are: 12,500 units

The fixed overhead shown above comprises both general and specific fixed overhead costs. The general fixed overhead cost has been absorbed on the basis of direct labour cost. The specific fixed cost relating only to product M2 is $2,500 per annum.

Calculate the maximum price that ABC would pay to an outside supplier for each unit of M2. $__________

LONG-TERM DECISION MAKING

181 R is due to receive \$20,000 in 5 years' time. Using a cost of capital of 7.6%, the discount factor will be closest to:

A 0.059

B 0.760

C 0.442

D 0.693

182 Consider the following statements about investment appraisal techniques. Identify if they relate to payback, net present value (NPV) or internal rate of return (IRR). Tick all that apply.

	Payback	**NPV**	**IRR**
Should ensure the maximisation of shareholder wealth			
Absolute measure			
Considers the time value of money			
A simple measure of risk			

183 LMN will receive \$25,000 in 6 years' time.

Calculate how much this is worth in today's terms, assuming an interest rate of 5.9%?

LMN will receive \$___________ in today's terms. (to the nearest \$).

184 Select the correct word to complete the sentences regarding investment appraisal methods.

A If the IRR is above/below the company's cost of capital, the project should be accepted.

B If NPV is positive/negative, accepting the project would increase shareholder value.

C If the payback period is greater/less than the target period, the project should be accepted.

185 STU has decided to expand its manufacturing facility. The cost of this expansion will be \$2.7m. Expected cash flows from the expansion are estimated as \$750,000 for the first 2 years and \$900,000 for the following 2 years.

Estimate the IRR of the project. ___________% (to 2 decimal places).

186 A project costing \$400,000 has the following expected cash flows.

Year	0	1	2	3	4	5
Annual cash flow (\$000)	(400)	200	150	100	70	40

The payback period for the project is _____ years _____ months (to the nearest month).

187 Two NPVs have been calculated for a project at two discount rates:

At discount rate 10%, NPV = $(3,451)

At discount rate 5%, NPV = $387

Estimate the IRR for the project.

A 10.1%

B 5.5%

C 9.5%

D 5.9%

188 A company has agreed to rent out unused office space for the next 10 years. It will receive a rent of $1,000 per annum. The first payment is due now. If interest rates are 8% then the present value of this rental income is equal to:

A $6,250

B $6,973

C $7,247

D $7,915

189 An investment of $150,000 is expected to generate cash inflows of $20,000 for the foreseeable future.

Estimate the IRR using the perpetuity method. ____________% (to one dp)

190 How much needs to be invested now at 5% to yield an annual income of $4,000 in perpetuity?

A $80,000

B $90,000

C $100,000

D $120,000

191 ABC is considering purchasing a new machine. The cost of the machine is $75,000. It is expected that the new machine will generate profits over the next 4 years as follows:

Year 1: $5,000

Year 2: $20,000

Year 3: $30,000

Year 4: $10,000

The machine will be sold at the end of the 4 years for $15,000. The above figures include a depreciation charge of $15,000 per year. ABC uses a 10% discount rate.

The NPV for the project will be:

A $22,960

B $33,205

C $70,495

D $80,740

192 Which TWO of the following statements are correct?

☐	A drawback of IRR is that it uses accounting figures rather than cash flows.
☐	Payback considers the whole life of the project.
☐	Calculations of IRR and Payback need to be compared to required targets in order to decide if the investment should be undertaken.
☐	NPV and Payback take account of the time value of money.
☐	NPV is an absolute measure while IRR is a relative measure.

193 An investment of $10 million is expected to generate net cash inflows of $3.5 million each year for the next 5 years.

Calculate the payback period for the investment (to the nearest month). ____________

194 A project requires an investment of $2.5 million to buy a new machine which is expected to generate net cash inflows of $750,000 each year for the next 4 years. It is estimated that the machine will be sold at the end of the project for $200,000. A discount of factor of 8% should be used.

Calculate the Net Present Value for the project. $____________

195 JKL is going to receive $1,000 per annum starting today and will receive five such payments.

If the rate of interest is 8%, calculate the present value of this income stream.
$____________

196 A company has been appraising a new project using the Net Present Value method. The calculation is shown below.

Year	Cash flow ($000)	Discount factor	Present value ($000)
0	(2,800)	1	(2,800)
1–5	620	4.100	2,542
5	150	0.713	107
		NPV =	**(151)**

Which THREE of the following statements are correct?

☐	The project should not be undertaken
☐	The project should be undertaken
☐	The discount rate used in the calculation was 7%
☐	The discount rate used in the calculation was 5%
☐	A higher discount rate would increase the NPV
☐	A lower discount rate would increase the NPV

197 Consider the following income streams.

Which is worth most, at present values, assuming an annual rate of interest of 12%?

A $1,200 one year from now

B $1,400 two years from now

C $1,600 three years from now

D $1,800 four years from now

198 How much would need to be invested today at 6% per annum to provide an annuity of $5,000 per annum for ten years commencing in five years' time?

A $5,000

B $19,000

C $29,150

D $39,420

199 **If a company invests $15,000 at an interest rate of 5%, how much will the investment be worth after three years? $__________ (to the nearest $)**

200 A project requires an investment of $60,000. It is anticipated that the cash inflows from the project will be $15,000 per annum for six years.

Using the annuity method, the IRR will be closest to?

A 4%

B 8%

C 13%

D 25%

Section 2

ANSWERS TO OBJECTIVE TEST QUESTIONS

THE CONTEXT OF MANAGEMENT ACCOUNTING

1

	Higher cost
	Less specialism
✓	Loss of control
	Duplication of effort
✓	Confidentiality risk

With outsourcing there can be a loss of control as management are not able to supervise the work on a day-to-day basis. This set-up can also create a confidentiality risk as important information can end up getting into the wrong hands. The other options are typical advantages of outsourcing.

2 The complete sentences are:

A The cash budget would be prepared by the **management** accountant.

B The cash flow statement would be prepared by the **financial** accountant.

C The statement of profit or loss would be prepared by the **financial** accountant.

The financial accountant is responsible for the preparation of the statutory accounts, comprising the statement of profit or loss, statement of financial position and cash flow statement. The management accountant is responsible for providing information to management to aid decision making. This information would include cash budgets.

3 The correct matching is:

Management accounting	Financial accounting
	Uses only historical data
Is carried out at the discretion of management	
Uses non-financial information	
Aids planning within the organisation	

4

✓	Information used by strategic management tends to be summarised
✓	Information used by strategic management tends to be forward looking
	Information used by operational management tends to contain estimates
	Information used by operational management tends to be required infrequently
	Information used by operational management tends to be from external sources

Operation level information is usually accurate, tends to be required frequently and tends to be from internal sources

5 C

Checking the accuracy of the financial statements would be an auditing role, which is not one of the main roles of management accounting.

6

	Preparing an annual budget for a cost centre
	Producing an investment appraisal calculation for a proposed new project
✓	Comparing the actual and expected results for a period and calculating the variances
	Advising management of the most profitable use of scarce resources
✓	Producing a monthly report of financial and non-financial performance measures for management

Preparing a budget is concerned with planning. Producing an investment appraisal calculation and advising the most profitable use of resources are decision making roles.

7 B

Strategic information is mainly used by senior management in an organisation.

Operational information is required frequently by its main users

Regular is not one of the characteristics of good information.

8 B

The five fundamental principles of the CIMA code of ethics are:

- Integrity
- Objectivity
- Professional competence and due care
- Confidentiality
- Professional behaviour

9 C

Being closer to the business needs is an advantage of having the management accounting located within the business unit. A, B and D are benefits from shared services centres (SSCs) or business process outsourcing (BPO).

10 B

Reporting is the main purpose of financial accounting. The main purposes of management accounting are planning, control and decision making.

11 The correct matching is shown below.

dedicated business partners	**shared services centres**	**business process outsourcing**
The finance staff are an integral part of the business they support	The whole finance function operates as one centre which provides for the finance needs of the whole company	The finance function is undertaken by a third party

12 B

Complete means that managers should be given all information that they require although this should not be excessive and understandable suggests that jargon and technical language should be limited.

In this case it would appear that managers are not getting all the information they require and that jargon is being used limiting the usefulness of the report.

13

	Making day-to-day decisions about the running of a department
✓	Defining the objectives of the company
✓	Deciding in which markets to operate
	Deciding about how to compete within their chosen markets
	Inventory control

Strategic level management would normally define the objectives of the company and make decisions about which markets to operate in. Tactical level managers would then decide how best to operate in these markets while operational level managers would make day-to-day decisions required in running their departments such as inventory control.

14 D

The four Global Management Accounting Principles are:

- Influence
- Trust
- Relevance
- Value

15 C

CIMA supports organisations in both the private and public sector. It focuses on the needs of businesses, no matter what type of business

16 C

Professional competence and due care requires accountants to have an ongoing commitment to their level of professional knowledge and skill and to put themselves forward for a role which they do not have the correct knowledge and experience to undertake would be breaching this principle.

17 The complete sentences are shown below:

- The decision on how much inventory of clothing to carry in each fitness centre would be made at the **operational** level.
- The decision to move into the fitness clothing industry would be made at the **strategic** level.
- The decision on the range of clothing to sell and the pricing of the range would be made at the **tactical** level.

Decisions on what industry to operate in would normally be made at the strategic level. Decisions on how to compete within that industry would normally be made at the tactical level and day-to-day decisions would normally be made at the operational level.

18

	Management accounting tends to focus on the needs of external stakeholders.
✓	Management accounting information can be presented in any format.
	The main purpose of management accounting is to produce the statutory financial statements for the entity.
✓	Management accounting is carried out at the discretion of management.
	One of the key deliverables of management accounting is the cash flow statement.

Financial accounting tends to focus on the needs of external stakeholders, while management accounting focuses on the needs of management.

Management accounting information can be presented in any format, unlike financial accounting which must be presented in prescribed formats.

The main purpose of financial accounting is to produce the statutory financial statements for the entity, while the main purpose of management accounting is to provide information to management to assist them make decisions.

Management accounting is carried out at the discretion of management to assist them in decision making, unlike financial accounting which is a statutory requirement.

One of the key deliverables of financial accounting is the cash flow statement, along with the statement of financial position and the statement of profit or loss.

19 The complete sentences are:

The role of the management accountant has changed over the years. Where the role used to be mainly concerned with **reporting** performance it is now more concerned about **enhancing** performance.

Management accountants are now seen as value-adding business partners. Their main purpose is providing **information** to managers for the purposes of **planning**, **control** and **decision making**.

20

✓	Objectivity
	Trust
	Influence
✓	Integrity
✓	Confidentiality

The five fundamental principles are

- Integrity
- Objectivity
- Professional competence and due care
- Confidentiality
- Professional behaviour

COSTING

COST IDENTIFICATION AND CLASSIFICATION

21 The complete sentences are:

Fixed costs are conventionally deemed to be constant in total when production volume changes

With **stepped** costs the total cost increases in steps as the level of activity increases

Examples of a **semi-variable** cost would be electricity and gas

Variable costs are conventionally deemed to be constant per unit of output

22 C

On an individual basis, materials, labour and direct expenses are direct costs but collectively, they are known as prime costs.

23 The correct matching is:

The cost of the market research	**Irrelevant**
The depreciation charge on the new machine	**Irrelevant**
Rental of factory space	**Relevant**
Labour costs in production department	**Irrelevant**

The only relevant cost is the loss of the rental income. This is an opportunity cost.

The cost of the market research is a sunk cost and is therefore irrelevant. The depreciation charge on the new machine is a non-cash item and is therefore irrelevant. The labour costs in the production department are irrelevant as the production can be carried out by the existing staff at no extra cost.

24 **$42 per unit**

Prime costs are direct costs, and exclude all overheads.

Prime cost = $(10 + 29 + 3) = **$42 per unit**.

25 **B**

Direct costs are those costs which can be economically identified with a single cost unit.

26 **D**

Although total fixed costs are the same at all levels of activity, the fixed cost per unit falls as the activity level increases. The unit cost does not fall in a straight line, but in a curve as shown in the question.

27

	The depreciation of stores equipment
✓	The hire of a machine for a specific job
✓	Royalty paid for each unit of a product produced
	Factory rent
	Factory supervisor's salary

Depreciation, factory rent and the factory supervisor's salary are indirect costs because they cannot be identified with a specific cost unit.

28 **B**

Managers are not usually classified as direct labour, because their salary cost cannot be traced to specific cost units.

29 **C**

The variable cost per unit is deemed to be constant as activity level changes. This diagram could also show total fixed costs.

30 The correct matching is:

A Hotel – **Bed-night**

B University – **Student**

C Bakery – **Batch of 20 pies**

D Accounting practice – **Chargeable hour**

31 The correct matching is:

A Variable cost per unit – **graph 1**

B Total fixed cost – **graph 1**

C Stepped fixed costs – **graph 3**

D Total variable cost – **graph 2**

E Total semi-variable cost – **graph 4**

32 The complete sentences are:

- The salary of an HR manager in a car servicing company would be classified as **indirect** labour.
- The salary of a bricklayer in a construction company would be classified as **direct** labour.
- The salary of a factory supervisor in a production company would be classified as **indirect** labour.

The wages of the bricklayer would be able to be identified with a specific cost unit therefore this would be a direct labour cost. The wages paid to the HR manager and the factory supervisor cannot be identified with specific cost units and would therefore be classified as indirect labour costs.

33 **B**

As the factory operation grows, additional supervisors will be employed.

34 The complete sentences are:

As volume decreases, fixed cost per unit will **increase** and total fixed costs will **stay the same**.

As volume decreases, variable cost per unit will **stay the same** and total variable costs will **decrease.**

35 The complete sentences are:

A unit of product or service in relation to which costs are ascertained is known as a **cost unit**.

A production or service location, a function, an activity or an item of equipment for which costs are accumulated is known as a **cost centre**.

Anything for which costs can be ascertained is known as a **cost object**.

ANALYSING AND PREDICTING COSTS

36 **D** **Variable**

E **Semi-variable**

F **Fixed**

G **Variable**

Cost D: (2,100 ÷ 300) = $7, (3,850 ÷ 550) = $7 so cost D is a variable cost

Cost E: (5,340 ÷ 300) = $17.80, (6,040 ÷ 550) = $10.98 so cost E is a semi-variable cost

Since cost F is constant for both activity levels it is a fixed cost.

Cost G: (360 ÷ 300) = $1.20, (660 ÷ 550) = $1.20 so cost G is a variable cost

37 **D**

The calculation is as follows:

Total overhead for 18,000 hours	$380,000
Variable overhead (18,000 × $ 5)	$90,000
Fixed overhead	$290,000

38

✓	89% of the variation in production costs from one month to the next can be explained by corresponding variation in output.
	Costs increase as output increases.
✓	The linear relationship between output and costs is very strong.
	An increase of 100% in output is associated with an increase of 89% in costs.
	An increase of 89% in output is associated with an increase of 100% in costs.

A coefficient of determination between output and production costs, tells us that 89% of the variation in production costs from one month to the next can be explained by corresponding variation in output. It also tells us that the linear relationship between output and costs is very strong. Only a positive correlation can tell us that costs increase as output increases and we cannot assume this from the coefficient of determination.

39 **C**

	Units	Cost
Highest month	900	$2,000
Lowest month	400	$1,000
Difference	500	$1,000

Variable cost per unit = ($1,000 ÷ 500) = $2.

Variable cost for September = (650 × $2) = $1,300.

40 The variable cost per unit is **$3.50.**

	Units	**Cost**
High	18,500	$251,750
Low	17,000	$246,500
Difference	1,500	$5,250

Variable cost per unit = ($5,250 ÷ 1,500) = $3.50.

41 **C**

Do not be confused by the use of the y and x notation. You simply need to think through how to calculate the total cost of a semi-variable cost.

Total semi-variable cost = fixed cost + (variable cost per unit × no. of units)

So, the total photocopying cost for a month can be shown as:

$y = 300 + 0.02x$

42 **A**

	Calls	**Cost**
Highest	1,800	$4,600
Lowest	800	$2,100
Difference	1,000	$2,500

Variable cost = $2,500 ÷ 1,000 = $2.50 per call

Fixed cost (using 800 calls) = Total cost – variable cost

= $2,100 – (800 × $2.50)

= $2,100 – $2,000 = $100

So fixed cost = $100 and variable cost = $2.50 per call.

43 **C**

The correlation coefficient calculated shows that there is a strong positive correlation between the number of holidays booked and the number of complaints. To explain how much of the change in the number of complaints is as a result of changes in the number of holidays booked, you would use the coefficient of determination. This is calculated as r^2. In this case the coefficient of determination would be $0.969^2 = 0.939$. Using this measure we can say that 93.9% of the observed changes in the number of complaints can be explained by the changes in the number of holidays booked and 6.1% can be explained by other factors.

44 **C**

The scatter graph shows a strong positive relationship therefore the correlation coefficient for this graph would be approximately 0.8

45 The cost of 80 cleaning jobs will be **$2,376**

	Calls	Cost
Highest	60	$2,282
Lowest	50	$2,235
Difference	10	$47

Variable cost = $47 ÷ 10 = $4.70 per job

Fixed cost (using 60 job) = Total cost – variable cost

= $2,282 – (60 × $4.70) = $2,282 – $282 = $2,000

So fixed cost = $2,000 and variable cost = $4.70 per job.

For 80 cleaning jobs the total cost will be $2,000 + (80 × $4.70) = $2.376

OVERHEAD ANALYSIS

46 The total overhead cost of the Finishing department will be **$190,000**

	Machining	**Finishing**	**Stores**	**Maintenance**
	$000	$000	$000	$000
Apportioned costs	190.00	175.00	30.00	25.00
Stores apportionment	18.00	9.00	(30.00)	3.00
Maintenance apportionment	21.00	5.60	1.40	(28.00)
Stores apportionment	0.84	0.42	(1.40)	0.14
Maintenance apportionment	0.11	0.03	–	(0.14)
Total	229.95	190.05		

47 **C**

Machine hour rate = $99,000 ÷ 22,000 = $4.50 per machine hour

48 The complete sentences are:

Overhead **apportionment** involves spreading common costs over cost centres on the basis of benefit received.

Overhead **reapportionment** involves sharing the costs of service cost centres to production cost centres.

49 The budgeted overhead absorption rate per chargeable labour hour was **$72.45**

	$
Actual overheads incurred	26,700
Over absorption	2,280
Overhead absorbed by actual hours	28,980
Overhead rate per hour = $28,980/400	$72.45

50 D

$$\frac{\text{Budgeted overheads}}{\text{Budgeted labour hours}} = \frac{\$148,750}{8,500} = \$17.50$$

Actual hours × absorption rate

= 7,928 × $17.50 = $138,740

	$
Actual overhead	146,200
Amount absorbed	138,740
Under absorption	7,460

51 A

Overheads absorbed (10,980 × $23)	$252,540
Actual overheads	$254,692
Overheads were under-absorbed by	$2,152

52 Cost to be apportioned to machining department is **$8,360**

Maintenance cost per hour in the three cost centres = $10,340 ÷ (3,800 + 850 + 50) = $2.20. Cost to be apportioned to machining department = ($2.20 × 3,800 hours) = $8,360

53 The overhead absorption rate was **$5 per unit**.

	$
Actual overheads	500,000
Over absorption	50,000
Overhead absorbed	550,000

Overhead absorption rate = $550,000/110,000 units = $5.

54 Actual labour hours were **3,600** hours.

	$
Actual overheads	20,000
Under-absorbed overhead	2,000
Absorbed overheads	18,000

Absorption rate = $25,000 ÷ 5,000 hours = $5 per labour hour.

Actual labour hours = $18,000 ÷ $5 = $3,600

55 Total overhead for department X is **$348,250.**

R = 140,000 + 0.3S (1)

S = 113,000 + 0.2R (2)

Substitute (1) in equation (2):

S = 113,000 + 0.2 (140,000 + 0.3S)

S = 113,000 + 28,000 + 0.06S

0.94S = 141,000

S = 150,000

Substituting this into equation (1)

R = 140,000 + (0.3 × 150,000) = 185,000

Total overheads for department X

= 220,000 + (45% × 185,000) + (30% × 150,000) = $348,250.

56

✓	Overheads were under absorbed
	Overheads were over absorbed
✓	The overhead absorption rate was $5.00 per labour hour
	The overhead absorption rate was $5.28 per labour hour
	The amount of the over/under absorption was $2,500
✓	The amount of the over/under absorption was $3,000

Overhead absorption rate = 55,000/11,000 = $5 per labour hour

Overheads absorbed = (5 × 10,900)	$54,500
Actual overheads	$57,500
Under absorption	$3,000

57 The overhead absorption rate per unit is **$12.50**.

Total overheads = $25,000

Budgeted units = 2,000

Overhead per unit = $25,000/2,000 = $12.50.

Since the company makes only one product, the unit fixed cost can be calculated simply by dividing total overhead by the production volume in units. It is unnecessary to calculate an absorption rate per hour for each department.

58 The fixed overhead cost of one product H would be **$20.00**.

Cutting department:

Budgeted hours = (6,000 × 0.05) + (6,000 × 0.10) = 900 hours

Absorption rate for the cutting department = $120,000/900 = $133.33.

Stitching department:

Budgeted hours = (6,000 × 0.20) + (6,000 × 0.25) = 2,700 hours

Absorption rate for the cutting department = $72,000/2,700 = $26.67.

Fixed overhead cost of one unit of product H = (0.10 × $133.33) + (0.25 × $26.67) = $20.

59 **A**

Overheads actually absorbed	=	$343,825 + $14,025
	=	$357,850
Overhead absorption rate	=	$357, 850 ÷ 21,050 hours = $17 per hour
Budgeted labour hours	=	$340,000 ÷ $17 = 20,000 hours

60

✓	Production activity higher than budget and actual fixed overhead expenditure as budgeted.
	Production activity lower than budget and actual fixed overhead expenditure as budgeted.
	Production activity lower than budget and actual fixed overhead expenditure higher than budget.
	Production activity as budgeted and actual fixed overhead expenditure more than budget.
✓	Production activity as budgeted and actual fixed overhead expenditure less than budget.

The combinations given in the first and last options will cause the overhead absorbed to be higher than the actual overhead incurred. The combinations in the remaining options will cause an under-absorption.

MARGINAL AND ABSORPTION COSTING

61 B

If profit margin is 20%, unit cost is 80% of the sales price, so with a selling price of $150, costs must be $120 and profit $30. Mark-up is based on costs. If costs are $120 and selling price is $150, then costs have been marked-up by 25%.

This is summarised below:

	$	**Margin %**	**Mark-up %**
Sales	150	100	125
Costs	120	80	100
Profit	30	20	25

62 A

	$
Selling price	220
Variable production costs	45
Other variable costs	20
Contribution per unit	155
× units	× 5,000
Total contribution	775,000
Less fixed overheads	275,000
Profit	500,000

63 The price to be charged for the job is **$23,446**.

	$
Direct material	10,650
Direct labour	3,260
Prime cost	13,910
Mark up on prime cost (60%)	8,346
Production overhead (140 × $8.50)	1,190
	23,446

64

	The prime cost is $25
	If the selling price was $65, the contribution would be $40
	20% mark-up on total cost would give a selling price of $60
✓	25% mark-up on total production cost would give a selling price of $40
✓	15% margin would give a selling price of $60

	$
Direct material	12
Direct labour	8
Prime cost	20
Variable production overhead	5
Fixed production costs	7
Total production cost	32
Non production costs	19
Total cost	51

If the selling price was $65, the contribution would be (65 – 12 – 8 – 5 – 4) = $36

20% mark-up on total cost would give a selling price of $51 × 1.2 = $61.20

25% mark-up on total production cost would give a selling price of $32 × 1.25 = $40

15% margin would give a selling price of $51 ÷ 0.85 = $60

65 **C**

In marginal costing, inventory is valued at marginal (variable) cost while in absorption costing inventory is valued at full production cost.

When inventory levels are decreasing, marginal costing will give the higher profit. When inventory levels are increasing, absorption costing will give the higher profit.

66 The profit mark-up is **55%.**

Cost of sales = opening inventory + purchases – closing inventory

= $(5,500 + 38,000 – 7,500)

= $36,000.

$36,000 + Mark-up = $55,800

Mark-up = $19,800

Mark-up % = 19,800 ÷ 36,000 × 100% = 55%

67 The selling price per unit is **$129.60.**

	$ per unit
Direct material cost	22.00
Direct labour cost	65.00
Production overhead absorbed (5 hours × $3)	15.00
Total production cost	102.00
Mark-up for non-production costs (8% × $102)	8.16
Full cost	110.16
Profit mark-up (15/85 × $110.16)	19.44
Selling price	129.60

68 C

There was an increase in inventory in the period therefore the absorption costing profit is higher than the marginal costing profit.

	$
Marginal costing profit	72,300
Change in inventory × OAR (750 – 300) × $5	2,250
Absorption costing profit	**74,550**

69 C

	$
Prime cost	6,840
Fixed overhead ($300,000/60,000) × 156 hours	780
Total production cost	7,620
Profit 20% × 7,620	1,524
Job price	9,144

70 D

	$
Marginal costing profit	50,400
Change in inventory × OAR (14,100 – 12,600) × OAR	?
Absorption costing profit	60,150

? = $60,150 – $50,400 = $9,750

OAR = $9,750 ÷ (14,100 – 12,600) = $6.50

PLANNING AND CONTROL

BUDGETING

71 The variable overhead variance for the month is **$450 favourable**.

Variable overhead flexed budget = $5,000 ÷ 10,000 × 9,500 = $4,750.

Variance = $4,750 – $4,300 = $450 favourable

72 The fixed overhead variance for the month is **$200 adverse**.

Variance = $5,000 – $5,200 = $200 adverse.

73 C

Production budget = Sales – opening inventory + closing inventory.

74 C

Budgetary slack is the intentional overestimating of costs or underestimating of revenues to ensure that the budget is achievable.

75 B

	$
January sales (20% × 95% × $50,000)	9,500
December sales (60% × $100,000)	60,000
November sales (10% × $60,000)	6,000
	75,500

76 **C**

Actual overheads	$300,000
Adverse variance	$18,000
Budgeted expenditure	$282,000
Less: Budgeted fixed costs	$87,000
Budgeted variable costs	$195,000

Budgeted variable cost per unit = $195,000 ÷ 162,500 = $1.20

77 Budgeted fixed costs were **$37,500**

	$
Total overheads	98,000
Less: Fixed overheads over budget	11,000
Budgeted overheads for 18,000 units	87,000
Less: Variable overheads (18,000 × $2.75)	49,500
Budgeted fixed overhead	37,500

78 The raw material usage budget for February is **7,600kg.**

Production for February is 3,800 units. Each unit requires 2kg of raw material therefore the raw material usage budget for February is 3,800 × 2kg = 7,600kg.

79 The correct matching is:

A With this approach, the budget is prepared by senior managers – **Imposed**

B A disadvantage of this approach is that it can be very time consuming as all budgeted costs must be justified by the expected benefits – **Zero-based**

C This approach is more likely to motivate managers as they are involved in the budget preparation – **Participative**

D With this approach the budget is continuously updated – **Rolling**

80 **C**

Material required for 1,000 units = 1,000 × 5 kg = 5,000 kg.

Input required = 5,000 kg ÷ 0.8 = 6,250 kg

Purchases required = 6,250 – 200 + 100 = 6,150 kg

81 B

Total variance = volume variance + expenditure variance.

Total variance = $7,500 A + $3,100 F = $4,400 A

82 The budget cost allowance for maintenance costs is **$214,394.**

Hours	$
8,520	216,440
8,300	211,600
220	4,840

Variable maintenance cost per hour = $4,840 ÷ 220 = $22

Fixed maintenance cost = $216,440 – (8,520 hours × $22) = $29,000

Budget cost allowance for 8,427 hours = $29,000 + (8,427 × $22) = $214,394

83 The complete sentences are:

The **principal budget factor** is the limiting factor which determines all other budgets.

A **budget centre** is a section in an organisation for which control may be exercised and budgets prepared.

The objective of a **cash budget** is to anticipate any shortages or surpluses which may arise in the future.

A **forecast** is a prediction of what is expected to happen, a **budget** is a quantified formal plan that the organisation is aiming to achieve.

84 The complete sentences are:

A A **flexible** budget is designed to change as volume of activity changes.

B **Fixed** budgets take no account of production shortfalls.

C **Flexible** budgets are useful for control purposes while **fixed** budgets are more useful for planning.

STANDARD COSTING AND VARIANCE ANALYSIS

85 The complete sentences are:

1 A standard established for use over a long period of time is known as a **basic** standard.

2 A standard which is set taking account of efficiency levels is known as an **attainable** standard.

3 A standard based on the present performance levels is known as a **current** standard.

4 A standard which makes no allowance for inefficiency is known as an **ideal** standard.

86 B

Actual standard hours produced

	Hours
Product A (6 ÷ 60) × 5,100	510
Product B (10 ÷ 60) × 2,520	420
Product C (12 ÷ 60) × 3,150	630
	1,560

Budget standard hours = 1,560 × (100 ÷ 120) = 1,300

87 The actual contribution reported for the period was **$49,460**.

Adverse variances are deducted from the budgeted contribution to derive the actual contribution. Favourable variances are added because they would increase the contribution above the budgeted level.

$37,200 + $13,420 + $5,400 – $310 – $6,250 = $49,460.

88

	Both budgets and standards relate to the future
	Both budgets and standards must be quantified
✓	Both budgets and standards are expressed in aggregate terms
	Both budgets and standards are used in planning
✓	Both budgets and standards are expressed in unit terms

Standards are expressed in unit terms. Budgets are expressed in aggregate terms.

89

	favourable material usage
✓	adverse material usage
	favourable labour efficiency
✓	adverse labour efficiency
✓	favourable material price
	adverse material price

Inferior materials would likely result in an adverse material usage variance as there is likely to be more wastage as a result of the lower quality material. This would result in an adverse labour efficiency variance as dealing with low quality material and higher wastage would take more time.

The cheaper material would however result in a favourable material price variance.

90 A

Material purchased	$23,000
Price variance	+ $1,000
Usage variance	– $1,600
Standard price for actual production	$22,400

Actual production = $22,400/$32 = 700 units.

91 The material purchases in the period were **1,600 kg**

Standard quantity used (500 × 3kg)	1,500 kg
Usage variance	100 favourable
Materials used	1,400 kg
Opening inventory	(100)
Closing inventory	300
	1,600 kg

92 D

	$
8,200 kg should cost $0.80/kg	6,560
But did cost	6,888
Material price variance:	$328 (A)

870 units should use 8 kg each	6,960 kg
But did use	8,200 kg
Variance in kg	1,240 kg (A)
× standard price	$0.80
Material usage variance:	$992 (A)

93 D

	$
13,450 hours should have cost (× $12)	161,400
But did cost	159,400
Rate variance:	2,000 (F)

3,350 units should take (× 4 hours)	13,400 hours
But did take	13,450 hours
Variance in hours	50 (A)
× standard rate	$12.00
Efficiency variance:	$600 (A)

94 The sales price variance for the period was **$69,000 adverse**

46,000 units should sell for (× $34)	1,564,000
But did sell for	1,495,000
Sales price variance	69,000 adverse

95 The sales volume contribution variance for the period was **$14,000 favourable**

	Units
Budgeted sales volume	45,000
Actual sales volume	46,000
Sales volume variance in units	1,000 favourable
× standard contribution ($34 – $20)	$14
Sales volume contribution variance	$14,000 favourable

96

	The original standard hours were set too high
	The employees were more skilled than had been planned for
	Production volume was lower than budget
✓	An ideal standard was used for labour time
✓	A lower quality of material was used in production

An ideal standard makes no allowances for stoppages or idle time therefore it is most likely to result in an adverse labour efficiency variance. Lower quality material in production can lead to more stoppages and cause an adverse labour efficiency variance.

If the original standard time was set too high then the labour efficiency variance would be favourable. Employees who are more skilled are likely to work faster than standard, again resulting in a favourable efficiency variance. The efficiency variance is based on the expected time for the actual production volume therefore it is not affected by a difference between budgeted and actual production volume.

97

	Standard costing is a useful technique in dynamic environments.
✓	Standard costing is less useful in today's environment because simply achieving standard is no longer seen as acceptable.
✓	Standard costing has been criticised as it generally places emphasis on labour variances which is no longer appropriate with the increasing use of automated production techniques
	Standard costing is only really useful in manufacturing environments.
	Standard costing encourages companies to strive for continuous improvement.

98 The complete sentences are:

The direct labour rate variance is calculated by comparing the **actual** labour cost with the **standard** labour rate flexed by the **actual** number of hours worked.

An adverse direct labour rate variance suggests that the actual labour cost was **higher** than expected.

INTEGRATED ACCOUNTING SYSTEMS

99 A

In an integrated cost and financial accounting system, the accounting entries for production overhead absorbed would be:

DR WIP control account

CR overhead control account.

100 The correct entries are shown below:

	Debit	Credit	No entry in this account
Material usage variance account	✓		
Raw material control account			✓
Work-in-progress account		✓	

101 A

Debit	Credit
WIP control account	labour efficiency variance account

102 The cost analysis is shown:

	Direct labour costs	Indirect labour costs
Basic pay – direct employees	**55,000**	
Basic pay – indirect employees		**22,750**
Overtime – basic rate	**2,400**	
Overtime premium		**600**
Bonuses – direct employees		**1,000**
Bonuses – indirect employees		**1,500**

The overtime premium and the bonuses of the direct workers are treated as indirect costs as we are given no information that they are related to a specific job. All of the costs of the indirect workers are treated as indirect costs.

103 The completed sentences are:

1 If the overtime worked by direct employees was to complete a specific job for a customer, overtime premium would be treated as **direct** costs.

2 If the bonuses were paid for completion of a particular task, the bonuses would be treated as **direct** costs.

Where overtime is worked at the request of a customer, both the overtime at basic pay and the overtime premium would be treated as a direct cost. Where bonuses are paid specifically in relation to a certain task, then they can be treated as a direct cost of that task.

104

	CR Work in progress account
	DR Work in progress account
✓	DR Labour rate variance account
	CR Labour rate variance account
✓	CR Wages control account
	DR Wages control account

105

	If a company operates an integrated accounting system, they need to undertake a periodic reconciliation to ensure the cost and financial ledgers agree
✓	Control accounts are used as summary accounts to record the total entries for each ledger.
✓	Integrated accounting systems may not provide the quality of information required for management accounting purposes.
	Maintaining integrated accounting systems can result in duplication of work.
	With an integrated accounting system different profit figures can be calculated for financial and management accounting purposes.

If a company operates an integrated accounting system, they do not need to undertake a periodic reconciliation as only one system is used. This avoids the duplication which can be experienced if two separate systems are used. Because only one system is maintained the profit figures calculated for financial and management accounting purposes will be the same.

106 B

The entries for materials purchased on credit would be:

Debit Material control account

Credit Accounts Payable account

107 Raw materials brought into production is **$355,000**

WIP Control Account

Wages	$30,000	Finished goods	$350,000
Production overhead	$40,000	Balance carried forward	$75,000
Raw materials	**$355,000**		
	$425,000		$425,000

Raw materials is the balancing figure of $355,000.

PERFORMANCE MEASUREMENT

108 The complete table is shown below:

Department	Performance measure	Type of centre
A	ROCE	**Investment centre**
B	Total costs	**Cost centre**
C	Gross profit %	**Profit centre**

Cost centre managers are only responsible for costs. Profit centre managers are also responsible for revenues. Investment centre managers are responsible for both profit and investment.

109

✓	The learning and growth perspective focuses on the need for continual improvement of existing products and techniques
	The goal of reducing staff turnover would be used in the learning and growth perspective
	The balanced scorecard uses only non-financial performance measures
✓	The goal of increasing return on capital employed would be used in the financial perspective
	The four perspectives in the balance scorecard are customer, internal effectiveness, profit and learning and growth

The goal of reducing staff turnover would be used in the internal business processes perspective. The balanced scorecard uses both financial and non-financial performance measures.

The four perspectives in the balance scorecard are customer, internal business processes, financial and learning and growth

110

	XYZ has failed to succeed in meeting any of its goals
✓	XYZ's cost per member in Year 1 was $1,600
✓	XYZ's number of complaints per member in Year 2 was 0.062
	XYZ's total cost has increased by 3.4%
	XYZ's number of total members has increased by 1.47%

XYZ has failed to reduce the number of customer complaints or to increase the number of new members but it has succeeded in reducing the cost per member. This reduced from $1,600 in Year 1 to $1,570 in Year 2.

XYZ's total cost has increased by 1.47% and XYZ's number of total members has increased by 3.4%

111 The complete sentences are:

A XYZ's number of complaints has increased and its number of complaints per member has **decreased**.

B XYZ's total cost has **increased** and its total cost per member has **decreased**.

C XYZ's number of new members has **decreased** and its number of repeat members has **increased**.

112 B

Meals served is not an example of a composite cost unit since it only takes into account one factor.

113 C

While all of these measures could be used, the most appropriate cost unit in this example is the tonne mile.

114 A

R is only responsible for costs.

115 The completed balanced scorecard diagram is:

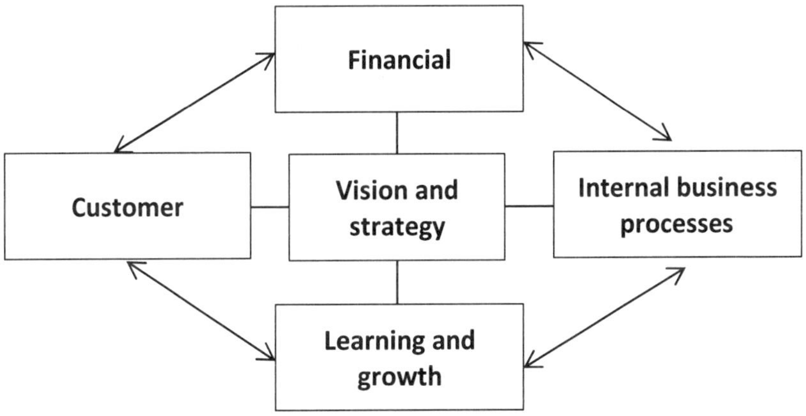

116 The ROCE for CDE is **17.1%** and for PQR is **8.3%**

$$\text{ROCE \%} = \frac{\text{Net (operating) margin}}{\text{Capital employed}}$$

CDE: ($1,300 ÷ $7,600) = 17.1%

PQR: ($700 ÷ $8,400) = 8.3%

117 The operating margin % for CDE is **14.8%** and for PQR is **7.7%**

$$\text{Net (operating) margin \%} = \frac{\text{Net (operating) margin}}{\text{Sales revenue}}$$

CDE: ($1,300 ÷ $8,800) = 14.8%

PQR: ($700 ÷ $9,100) = 7.7%

PREPARING ACCOUNTS AND REPORTS FOR MANAGEMENT

118 D

	Job 1	Job 2	Total
	$	$	$
Opening WIP	8,500	–	8,500
Materials	17,150	29,025	46,175
Labour	12,500	23,000	35,500
Overheads	43,750	80,500	124,250
Closing WIP	81,900	132,525	214,425

Workings:

Total labour for period = $(12,500 + 23,000 + 4,500) = $40,000

Overhead absorption rate = $140,000 ÷ $40,000 = 350% of labour cost

119 C

	Job 3
	$
Opening WIP	20,000.00
Material	5,000.00
Labour	4,500.00
Overheads (350% × $4,500)	15,750.00
Total production costs	45,250.00
Profit 25%	11,312.50
Selling price of 1,500 unit	56,562.50
Selling price per unit	$37.71

120 B

$50 ÷ (1 – 0.4) = $83.33

121 D

Senior	86 hours at $20	$1,720
Junior	220 hours at $15	$3,300
Overheads	306 hours at $12.50	$3,825
Total cost		$8,845
Mark-up	(40%)	$3,538
Selling price		$12,383

122 The gross profit for the period was **$34,500**

Senior	750 hours at $20	$15,000
Junior	2,250 hours at $15	$33,750
Overheads	3,000 hours at $12.50	$37,500
Total cost		$86,250
Profit	(40% mark-up)	$34,500

123 The price to be quoted for the job is **$2,600**

The profit margin is expressed as a percentage of the selling price.

Therefore selling price = $2,080 ÷ (1 – 0.2) = $2,600

124 **D**

Direct cost of producing 100 cards:

	$
Artwork	40
Machine setting (3hrs × $15)	45
Paper ($2 × 10)	20
Ink	10
Wages (1hr × $10)	10
	$125

125 The selling price for 200 cards is **$283**

	$
Artwork	40
Machine setting (3hrs × $15)	45
Paper ($2 × 20)	40
Ink	20
Wages (2hr × $10)	20
	165
Overheads (165 × 20%)	33
	198
Profit (30 ÷ 70 ×198)	85
Selling price	283

126 The correct matching is shown:

Each service is unique and cannot usually be repeated in the same way.	**Variability**
Services cannot be stored for use at a later date.	**Perishability**
Services generally have simultaneous production and consumption.	**Inseparability**
Services often have few, if any, physical attributes.	**Intangibility**

127 The contribution for Division A is **$170,000**

Variable cost for Division A = (1 ÷ 10) × $300,000 = $30,000

Contribution = Sales – variable cost

= $200,000 – $30,000 = $170,000

128 The contribution per km for Division B is **$1.80**

Variable cost for Division B = (4 ÷ 10) × $300,000 = $120,000

Contribution = Sales – variable cost

= $300,000 – $120,000 = $180,000

Distance travelled = 100,000 km

Contribution per km = ($180,000 ÷ 100,000) = $1.80

129 The complete sentences are:

- If a hospital compared the current waiting time for patients against the target time, this would be a measure of **effectiveness**.
- If a school compared the % passes for actual exam results compared to target exam results, this would be a measure of **effectiveness**.
- If a university measured the % of graduates who found full time employment within a year of graduating, this would be a measure of **effectiveness**.

130

✓	Actual material cost
	Actual manufacturing overheads
✓	Absorbed manufacturing overheads
	Budgeted labour cost
	Budgeted material cost

Overhead cost is absorbed into job costs using a pre-determined absorption rate. It is not usually possible to identify the actual manufacturing overhead costs related to specific jobs.

DECISION MAKING

RISK – SUMMARISING AND ANALYSING DATA

131 **B** and **C**

	8 members of staff worked less than 20 games
✓	XYZ have 20 members of staff in total
✓	4 members of staff worked 30 or more games
	The most popular number of games to have worked is 25 – 29
	Only 4 members of staff could have worked all 40 games

7 members of staff worked less than 20 games. The most popular number of games to have worked is 20 – 24. Only 1 member of staff could have worked all 40 games.

132 The angle for Wheat would be **155°** and the angle for Oats would be **43°**

Wheat angle = (43 ÷ 100) × 360 = 155°

Oats angle = (12 ÷ 100) × 360 = 43°

133 Mean = **125 seconds**

Time taken (mid-point)	f	fx	fx^2
107.5	2	215.00	23,112.50
112.5	5	562.50	63,281.25
117.5	4	470.00	55,225.00
122.5	8	980.00	120,050.00
127.5	10	1,275.00	162,562.50
132.5	5	662.50	87,781.25
137.5	4	550.00	75,625.00
142.5	2	285.00	40,612.50
	40	5,000.00	628,250.00

Mean = Σfx ÷ Σf = 5,000 ÷ 40 = 125 seconds

134 Standard deviation = **9.01**

$$S = \sqrt{\frac{\Sigma fx^2}{\Sigma f} - \left(\frac{\Sigma fx}{\Sigma f}\right)^2}$$

$$\text{Standard deviation} = \sqrt{\frac{628{,}250}{40} - \left(\frac{5{,}000}{40}\right)^2} = 9.01$$

135 **D**

136 B

To be correctly presented, the histogram must show the relationship of the rectangles to the frequencies by reference to the area of each rectangle.

137 B

There are 360 degrees in a circle

So (90 ÷ 360) × $550,000 = $137,500

138 C

Cumulative frequencies are plotted against the upper class boundaries.

139 x = **24kg**

Mean = 20 kg

Samples size = 10

so 15 + *x* + 22 + 14 + 21 + 15 + 20 + *x* + 18 + 27 = 200

so 152 + 2*x* = 200

2x = 48

x = 24

140 The complete sentences are:

- The **mode** is the value which appears with the highest frequency
- The **mean** is calculated by adding all of the values and dividing the total by the number of values
- The **median** is the middle of a set of values

141 The standard deviation is **1.11.**

Orders (x)	Frequency	fx	fx^2
1	3	3	3
2	5	10	20
3	12	36	108
4	14	56	224
5	6	30	150
Total	40	135	505

$$S = \sqrt{\frac{\Sigma fx^2}{\Sigma f} - \left(\frac{\Sigma fx}{\Sigma f}\right)^2}$$

$$S = \sqrt{\frac{505}{40} - \left(\frac{135}{40}\right)^2}$$

$$= \sqrt{12.63 - 11.39}$$

$$= \sqrt{1.24} = 1.11$$

142 C

To make calculation easier subtract 500

$$\text{So } 500 = \frac{4+6+1+5+7+6+4+8+3+5+2+4}{12}$$

$$= 500 + \frac{55}{12} = 504.6$$

143 B

Arranging in numerical order we have

501, 502, 503, 504, 504, 504, 505, 505, 506, 506, 507, 508

Median = (504 + 505) ÷ 2 = 504.5

144 A

The modal weight is 504 since it appears more times than any other

145 The complete frequency distribution is shown below

Time	**Frequency**
105 > 110	2
110 > 115	**6**
115 > 120	4
120 > **125**	8
125 > 130	**9**
130 > 135	5
135 > **140**	4
140 > 145	2

146 The correct matching is:

A Data has to be arranged in order of size which is time consuming – **Median**

B It may give undue weight or be influenced by extreme values – **Mean**

C Data has to be arranged to ascertain which figure appears the most often – **Mode**

The arithmetic mean is calculated by taking the total value of all items divided by the total number of items. The median is the value of the middle item in a distribution once all the items have been arranged in order of magnitude. The mode is the value that occurs most frequently amongst all the items in the distribution.

RISK – PROBABILITY

147 The company should order **200 units**.

			Order	
Demand	**Probability**	100	200	300
100	0.25	10	(20)	(60)
200	0.40	10	30	0
300	0.35	10	30	80
	Expected value	10	17.5	13

Expected value for 100 units = (10 × 0.25) + (10 × 0.40) + (10 × 0.35) = 10

Expected value for 200 units = ((20) × 0.25) + (30 × 0.40) + (30 × 0.35) = 17.5

Expected value for 300 units = ((60) × 0.25) + (0 × 0.40) + (80 × 0.35) = 13

148

	It is symmetrical
	It is bell-shaped
✓	The area under the curve is equal to 0.5
	The mean is equal to the mode
✓	The mean is above the median

149 The complete payoff table is shown below:

		Order	
Demand	**4 boxes**	**5 boxes**	**6 boxes**
4 boxes	80	70	**60**
5 boxes	80	100	**90**
6 boxes	80	**100**	**120**

Calculate the profit for each outcome (total sales – total cost)

Order 4, demand 4: (4 × 30) – (4 × 10) = $80

Order 4, demand 5: $80

Order 4, demand 6: $80

Order 5, demand 4: (4 × 30) – (5 × 10) = $70

Order 5, demand 5: (5 × 30) – (5 × 10) = $100

Order 5, demand 6: $100

Order 6, demand 4: (4 × 30) – (6 × 10) = $60

Order 6, demand 5: (5 × 30) – (6 × 10) = $90

Order 6, demand 6: (6 × 30) – (6 × 10) = $120

150 The complete sentences are:

A When a situation can be repeated a number of times this is classed as **empirical** probability.

B Where estimates are made by individuals of the relative likelihood of events occurring, this is called **subjective** probability.

C When the probability can be applied to the population of outcomes this is called **exact** probability.

151 D

Expected value = ∑PX

= (0.3 × \$10) + (0.3 × \$50) + (0.4 × \$80)

= \$50

152 The council would make a **\$1,000 saving**

Cost of new machine = \$20,000

Expected saving = (0.2 × 40,000) + (0.5 × 20,000) + (0.3 × 10,000)

= \$8,000 + \$10,000 + \$3,000

= \$21,000

Based purely on expected value theory, the council should buy a new snow plough since they could expect to save \$1,000.

153 Expected profit from new product is **\$27,000**

(0.1 × \$100,000) + (0.5 × \$50,000) + (0.4 × –20,000)

= \$27,000

154 Ranking is

	Rank
Project A	**2**
Project B	**3**
Project C	**1**

Project A = (0.5 × \$5,000) + (0.5 × \$2,500)

= \$3,750

Project B = (0.3 × \$10,000) + (0.7 × \$1,000)

= \$3,700

Project C = (0.4 × \$6,000) + (0.6 × \$4,000)

= \$4,800

155 The percentage of total customers likely to recommend the organisation is **54%.**

The data from those customers that have responded would be extrapolated across all customers.

156 The probability of selecting at random a student who is non-binary and qualified is **12%.**

$\frac{20}{100} \times \frac{60}{100}$ or 12%

157 The probability that a car selected at random has a major defect is **16%.**

Where only percentage figures are given, it is easier to use an absolute number such as 1,000 and produce the following table:

	Factory X	Factory Y	Total
Fault	25	135	160
No fault	225	615	840
Total	250	750	1,000

The probability that a car selected at random has a major defect is 160 in 1,000 or 16%

158 A

The expected value of the investment is (0.4 × \$650,000) + (0.6 × \$450,000) = \$530,000

Current profit is \$500,000 therefore XYZ would be willing to pay up to \$30,000 for the investment.

159 B

$$Z = \frac{x - \mu}{\sigma}$$

$$Z = \frac{330 - 360}{15} = -2$$

From normal distribution table, look up 2, which gives 0.4772

So probability Z < \$330 = 0.5 – 0.4772 = 0.0228 or 2.3%

160 D

Required area is between 370 and 400

$$Z = \frac{400 - 360}{15} = 2.666$$

From table, Z = 2.666 gives 0.4962

$$Z = \frac{370 - 360}{15} = 0.667$$

From table, Z = 0.667 gives 0.2486

0.4962 – 0.2486 = 0.2476 or approximately 25%.

SHORT-TERM DECISION MAKING

161 Sales revenue to achieve a profit of $125,000 is **$450,000**

Sales revenue to achieve a profit of X = (Fixed cost + X) ÷ C/S ratio

= ($100,000 + $125,000) ÷ 0.5 = $450,000

162 D

The margin of safety can be determined once the chart has been constructed. It is not necessary to know the margin of safety in order to draw the chart.

163 A

Break-even point in sales revenue = Fixed costs ÷ C/S ratio

= $48,000 ÷ 0.4 = $120,000

Margin of safety in sales revenue = projected sales revenue – breakeven sales revenue

= $20,000

If selling price = $10 then the margin of safety in units is $20,000 ÷ $10 = 2,000 units.

164 A

The shaded area on the breakeven chart represents loss.

165

	The point where the total cost line cuts the vertical axis is the breakeven point on a traditional breakeven chart.
	The point where the total cost line cuts the horizontal axis is the breakeven point on a traditional breakeven chart.
✓	The point where the profit line cuts the horizontal axis is the breakeven point on a profit-volume chart.
	The point where the profit line cuts the vertical axis is the breakeven point on a profit-volume chart.
✓	The point where the total cost line and the total sales revenue line intersect is the breakeven point on a traditional breakeven chart.

The breakeven point on a traditional breakeven chart is where the total cost line and the total sales revenue line intersect.

The breakeven point on a profit-volume chart is where the profit line cuts the horizontal axis.

166 The profit line will cut the vertical axis at y = **–$30,000**.

This is the loss at zero activity, which is equal to the fixed cost.

167 C

Contribution to Sales Ratio:

Sales	$15,000
Variable Cost	$9,000
Contribution	$6,000

Contribution to sales = $6,000 ÷ $15,000 = 40%

168 B

Break-even point in sales revenue = Fixed costs ÷ C/S ratio

= $4,500 ÷ 0.4 = $11,250

Break-even in units = $11,250 ÷ $15 = 750 units

Margin of safety % = (1,000 – 750) ÷ 1,000 = 0.25 or 25%.

169 The contribution to sales ratio (C/S ratio) is **34%**.

Contribution per unit = $(53 – 24 – 8 – 3) = $18

Contribution to sales ratio = 18 ÷ 53 = 0.3396 or 34%

170 The margin of safety is **61%**.

Fixed costs = 7,200 × $7 = $50,400

Breakeven units = Fixed cost ÷ contribution per unit

= $50,400 ÷ $18 = 2,800 units

Margin of safety % = (7,200 – 2,800) ÷ 7,200 = 0.611 or 61%.

171 D

If X started her own business, she would be unable to continue in her current employment. She would therefore have to forgo her current salary. Her current salary is an opportunity cost of setting up her own business.

172 The relevant cost of the materials is **$500.**

Since the materials have no alternative use, they will not be replaced. Thus the relevant cost is the scrap proceeds forgone.

173 B

Units we could make from resources available:

Materials: $500 ÷ $5 =	100
Labour: 80 hours ÷ 2 hours =	40
Machine time: 148 hours ÷ 1 hour =	148

Therefore, labour is the limiting factor.

174

	The relevant cost of S is $4.80
✓	The relevant cost of S is $8.40
	The relevant cost of S is $3.60
	The relevant cost of T is $3.00
	The relevant cost of T is $4.20
✓	The relevant cost of T is $1.20

Material S: relevant cost = replacement cost	(2 × $4.20) =	$8.40
Material T: relevant cost = net realisable value	(3 × $0.40) =	$1.20

175 C

Rank the products based on their contribution per labour hour:

	A	**B**	**C**
Contribution	$12.00	$5.50	$7.00
Labour hours	3	1	1
Contribution per labour hour	$4.00	$5.50	$7.00
Ranking	3	2	1

Labour available = 1,000 hours

This would be enough to make 1,000 units of C.

176 D

Let us take a numerical example using a sales value of $100:

	Original	**Change**	**New**
Selling price	100	+10%	110
Variable cost	60	–	60
Contribution/unit	40	+10	50

Percentage increase in contribution per unit = 10/40 = 25% increase.

177 B

Product	**X**	**Y**	**Z**
Contribution	$41.00	$54.00	$50.00
Materials kg	2	1	3
Contribution per LF	$20.50	$54	$16.66
Ranking	2	1	3

178 The complete sentences are:

- To maximise profit, RST should **5,000** units of X
- To maximise profit, RST should produce **3,200** units of Y
- To maximise profit, RST should produce **0** units of Z

Product	**X**	**Y**	**Z**
Contribution per unit	$24	$25	$30
Skilled labour hours per unit	0.40	0.50	0.75
Contribution per skilled labour hour	$60	$50	$40
Ranking	1	2	3

Available skilled labour hours	3,600
Make 5,000 X	(2,000)
	1,600
Make (1,600 ÷ 0.5) = 3,200 Y	(1,600)
	–

To maximise profit, produce 5,000 units of X and 3,200 units of Y. No units of Z should be produced.

179 D

	A	**B**	**C**	**D**
	$	$	$	$
Variable cost of manufacture	60	64	70	68
External purchase price	100	120	130	110
Cost of external purchase	(40)	(56)	(60)	(42)
Machine hours per unit	4	7	5	6
Cost of external purchase per hour	(10)	(8)	(12)	(7)

Buy in the component with the lowest cost per hour which is D.

180 The maximum price that ABC would pay to an outside supplier for each unit of M2 is **$4.60.**

Relevant production costs are those which are variable or, if fixed, are product specific. The relevant costs are therefore:

	$/unit
Variable production costs (3.00 + 1.00 + 0.40)	4.40
Fixed cost: $2,500/12,500 units	0.20
	4.60

LONG-TERM DECISION MAKING

181 D

Discount factor $= (1 + r)^{-n}$

$= (1 + 0.076)^{-5} = \mathbf{0.693}$

182

	Payback	NPV	IRR
Should ensure the maximisation of shareholder wealth		✓	✓
Absolute measure		✓	
Considers the time value of money		✓	✓
A simple measure of risk	✓		

183 LMN will receive **$17,724.**

Present value = future value × discount factor

= $25,000 × $(1 + 0.059^{-6})$ = $17,724

184 The complete sentences are:

A If the IRR is **above** the company's cost of capital, the project should be accepted.

B If NPV is **positive**, accepting the project would increase shareholder value.

C If the payback period is **less** than the target period, the project should be accepted.

185 IRR = **8.31%**

Year	Cash flow ($000)	Discount factor (5%)	Present value ($000)	Discount factor (10%)	Present value ($000)
0	(2,700)	1	(2,700)	1	(2,700)
1	750	0.952	714.00	0.909	681.75
2	750	0.907	680.25	0.826	619.50
3	900	0.864	777.60	0.751	675.90
4	900	0.823	740.70	0.683	614.70
		NPV =	212.55	NPV =	(108.15)

The NPV has changed by $320.7k

The discount rate has changed by 5%

Therefore the NPV changes $64.14k for every 1% change in the discount rate ($320.7k / 5)

The IRR will be 5% + ($212.55k / $64.17k) = 5 + 3.31

IRR = 8.31%

The IRR could also have been estimated using the formula or graphical method.

186 The payback period is **2 years 6 months**

Year	**0**	**1**	**2**	**3**	**4**	**5**
Annual cash flow ($000)	(400)	200	150	100	70	40
Cumulative cash flow	(400)	(200)	(50)	50	120	160

Payback is 2 years + (50/100 × 12) months = 2 years 6 months

187 B

The NPV has changed by $3,838

The discount rate has changed by 5%

Therefore the NPV changes $767.6 for every 1% change in the discount rate ($3,838 / 5)

The IRR will be 5% + ($387 / $767.6) = 5 + 0.5

IRR = 5.5%

The IRR could also have been estimated using the formula or graphical method.

188 C

PV = $1,000 × (1 + 6.247)

= $1,000 × 7.247

= $7,247

The income stream covers years 0 – 9. The 9 year annuity factor is 6.247 and the discount factor for year 0 is 1.

189 The IRR is **13.3%**

Where the investment generates perpetuity, the following method can be used to estimate the IRR:

$$\text{IRR} = \frac{\text{Annual cash inflow}}{\text{Initial investment}}$$

IRR = 20,000 ÷ 150,000 = 13.3%

190 A

$$\$4,000 \times \frac{1}{0.05} = \$80,000$$

191 B

Year	Cash flow ($)	Discount factor (10%)	Present value
0	(75,000)	1	(75,000)
1	20,000*	0.909	18,180
2	35,000*	0.826	28,910
3	45,000*	0.751	33,795
4	25,000* + 15,000 = 40,000	0.683	27,320
		NPV =	**33,205**

* depreciation of $15,000 must be added back to get the cash flows

192

	A drawback of IRR is that it uses accounting figures rather than cash flows.
	Payback considers the whole life of the project.
✓	Calculations of IRR and Payback need to be compared to required targets in order to decide if the investment should be undertaken.
	NPV and Payback take account of the time value of money.
✓	NPV is an absolute measure while IRR is a relative measure.

IRR uses cash flows.

Payback considers only up to the point that the initial investment is repaid; it ignores the cash flows after the payback period.

NPV takes account of the time value of money, but Payback does not.

193 The payback period is **2 years 11 months**.

Payback period for a constant annual cash flow = Initial investment ÷ annual cash flow

= 10,000,000/3,500,000 = 2.857

The payback period is 2 years + (0.857 × 12) months = 2 years 11 months.

194 The Net Present Value for the project is **$131,000.**

Year	Cash flow ($000)	Discount factor (8%)	Present value ($000)
0	(2,500)	1	(2,500)
1–4	750	3.312	2,484
4	200	0.735	147
		NPV =	131

195 The present value is **$4,312**

$1,000 × (1 + 3.312) = $4,312

The income stream covers years 0 – 4. The 4 year annuity factor is 3.312 and the discount factor for year 0 is 1.

196

✓	The project should not be undertaken
	The project should be undertaken
✓	The discount rate used in the calculation was 7%
	The discount rate used in the calculation was 5%
	A higher discount rate would increase the NPV
✓	A lower discount rate would increase the NPV

The project has a negative NPV therefore it should not be undertaken.

The discount rate used in the calculation can be found by looking up the present value tables. Look along the 5 year row until you find 0.735. This appears in the 7% column. To confirm, check that 3.312 is the 7%, 5 year annuity factor.

A lower discount rate would increase the NPV. A lower discount rate will give a higher discount factor and therefore a higher NPV.

197 D

$1,200/1.12 = $1,071

$1,400/(1.12)^2 = $1,116

$1,600/(1.12)^3 = $1,139

$1,800/(1.12)^4 = $1,144

198 C

From the cumulative present value table:

6% year 14	9.295	(coves years 1 – 14)
	3.465	(covers years 1 – 4)
	5.830	(covers years 5 – 14)

$5,000 × 5.830 = $29,150.

199 The investment would be worth **$17,364.**

Using compounding, the future value = present value × $(1 + r)^n$

Future value = $15,000 × 1.05^3

= $17,364

200 C

Year	Cash flow ($)	Discount factor	Present value ($)
0	(60,000)	1	(60,000)
1–6	15,000		60,000
		NPV =	0

The annuity method involves working backwards to estimate the discount factor.

The discount factor would be 60,000 ÷ 15,000 = 4

Look up the cumulative present value tables for year 6 and find the closest interest rate.

The interest rate 13% gives a discount factor of 3.998.

Section 3

PRACTICE ASSESSMENT QUESTIONS

1 The following cost data have been collected for four costs incurred by KLM at two activity levels.

Cost	Cost for 200 units	Cost for 250 units
A	$1,000	$1,000
B	$700	$875
C	$2,400	$2,500
D	$1,360	$1,700

Select the correct word to complete the sentences regarding the four costs:

Cost A is a fixed/variable/semi-variable cost.

Cost B is a fixed/variable/semi-variable cost.

Cost C is a fixed/variable/semi-variable cost.

Cost D is a fixed/variable/semi-variable cost.

2 **Which FOUR of the following are characteristics of good information?**

☐	Complete
☐	Concise
☐	Understandable
☐	Regular
☐	Responsible
☐	Timely
☐	Accurate
☐	Effective

3 PQR is due to receive perpetuity of $33,000 commencing immediately. Interest rates are 4.5%.

Calculate the present value of the cash flows from the perpetuity. $____________ (to the nearest $000)

The next two questions are based on the following data.

The table below relates to a number of CGMA candidates who recently sat the exam for a subject.

Location of student	Total number of scripts	Total number of passes
Europe	1,000	500
Outside of Europe	500	300

4 **If a student is selected at random what is the probability that they failed?**

A 33%

B 47%

C 50%

D 53%

5 **If a student is selected at random what is the probability of selecting a student located in Europe who failed?**

A 20%

B 25%

C 33%

D 50%

6 **The principal budget factor is the**

A factor which limits the activities of the organisation and is often the starting point in budget preparation

B budgeted revenue expected in a forthcoming period

C main budget into which all subsidiary budgets are consolidated

D overestimation of revenue budgets and underestimation of cost budgets, which operates as a safety margin against risk

7 In a period, a company had opening inventory of 31,000 units of Product G and closing inventory of 34,000 units. Profits based on marginal costing were $850,500 and profits based on absorption costing were $955,500.

If the budgeted fixed costs for the company for the period were $1,837,500, what was the budgeted level of activity?

A 24,300 units

B 27,300 units

C 52,500 units

D 65,000 units

8 XYZ operates an integrated cost accounting system. The Work-in-Progress Account at the end of the period showed the following information:

Work-in-Progress Account

	$		$
Material control	100,000	?	200,000
Wages control	75,000		
Factory overhead	50,000	Balance c/d	25,000
	225,000		225,000

What does the $200,000 credit entry represent?

A Cost of sales account

B Statement of profit or loss account

C Sales account

D Finished goods account

9 There are three departments in a factory.

Department A occupies 2,000 sq. metres

Department B occupies 2,500 sq. metres

Department C occupies 500 sq. metres

Annual rent = $40,000

The combined rent apportioned to Departments A and B is?

A $16,000

B $20,000

C $24,000

D $36,000

10 **In an integrated bookkeeping system, when the actual production overheads exceed the absorbed production overheads, the accounting entries to close off the production overhead account at the end of the period would be?**

Tick the required entries in each account.

	Debit	**Credit**	**No entry in this account**
Production overhead account			
Work in progress account			
Statement of profit or loss			

11 A company makes special assemblies to customers' orders and uses job costing. The data for the three jobs worked on during the last period are:

	AA10	BB15	CC20
	$	$	$
Opening WIP	26,800	42,790	0
Material added in period	17,275	0	18,500
Labour for period	14,500	3,500	24,600

The budgeted overhead for the period was $127,800

Calculate the amount of overhead to be added to job CC20 for the period. $__________

12 The following budgeted data have been prepared for a distribution company for the next year. The company uses tonne-miles as its cost unit.

Miles travelled	5,000
Tonnes carried	250
Number of drivers	25
Hours worked by drivers	3,750
Costs incurred	$3,500,000

Calculate the cost per tonne-mile for the year (to the nearest cent). $__________

13 A retailer can sell either Product A or Product B. Product A has a 40% chance of high sales and a 60% chance of low sales. High sales would yield a profit of $600. Low sales would yield a profit of $100. If Product B was sold there is a 60% chance of high sales and a 40% chance of low sales which would result in a profit of $400 or a loss of $50.

Which product should the retailer sell and what would be the expected profit?

A Product A $220

B Product B $220

C Product A $300

D Product B $300

14 A, B and C are managers in LMN. A is a profit centre manager, B is a cost centre manager and C is an investment centre manager.

On the following table, tick the items which each manager would be responsible for.

	A	B	C
Sales revenue			
Staff costs			
Capital investment			
Administration expenses			

15 RST is considering making an investment of $1.2m to launch a new product. It has undertaken some market research and has estimated that the new product could generate the following cash flows:

Year 1: $240,000

Year 2: $265,000

Year 3: $240,000

Year 4: $660,000

Year 5: $290,000

Calculate the payback period for the project and decide which of the following statements is true if RST requires payback within 4 years.

A Payback period is 3 years 9 months, therefore project should be undertaken

B Payback period is 3 years 9 months, therefore project should not be undertaken

C Payback period is 4 years 4 months, therefore project should be undertaken

D Payback period is 4 years 4 months, therefore project should not be undertaken

16 XYZ has two production departments (Machining and Assembly) and two service departments (Stores and Maintenance). The management accountant has just completed the allocation and apportionment of overheads to the four departments as shown:

	Machining	**Assembly**	**Stores**	**Maintenance**	**Total**
	$	$	$	$	$
Total	2,250,000	1,900,000	250,000	800,000	5,200,000

The service departments provide services as shown below:

	Machining	**Assembly**	**Stores**	**Maintenance**
Stores	30%	30%	–	40%
Maintenance	45%	30%	25%	–

Using the equation method, calculate the total overhead for the Machining department (to the nearest $000). $___________

17 **Which TWO of the following statements regarding the Global Management Accounting principles are true?**

☐	The principles should be used my management accountants as a guide to best practice.
☐	One of the key aims of the principles is to encourage integrated thinking within organisations.
☐	The principles are a statutory requirement for all members of CIMA.
☐	The four principles are influence, trust, reliability and value
☐	Two of the principles are integrity and objectivity

18 The budgeted contribution for RST last month was $32,000. The following variances were reported.

	$
Sales volume contribution	800 adverse
Material price	880 adverse
Material usage	822 favourable
Labour efficiency	129 favourable
Variable overhead efficiency	89 favourable

No other variances were reported for the month.

The actual contribution earned by RST last month was?

A $31,360

B $31,440

C $32,560

D $32,960

19 **Using some or all of the following terms, complete the sentences below. Terms can be used more than once.**

- Fixed
- Variable
- Increases
- Reduces

Total _______cost, within a relevant range, is not affected by changes in activity levels.

Fixed cost per unit _______ as the activity level increases.

Total variable cost ______as the activity level increases.

On a graph showing activity level on the x axis and cost on the y axis, ______ cost per unit would be shown as a horizontal line.

20 LMN is due to receive a 15 year annuity of $3,000 starting at once.

If interest rates are 6%, calculate the present value of the cash flows from the annuity.
$___________ (to the nearest $)

21 The following scatter graph has been prepared for the costs incurred by an organisation that delivers hot meals to the elderly in their homes.

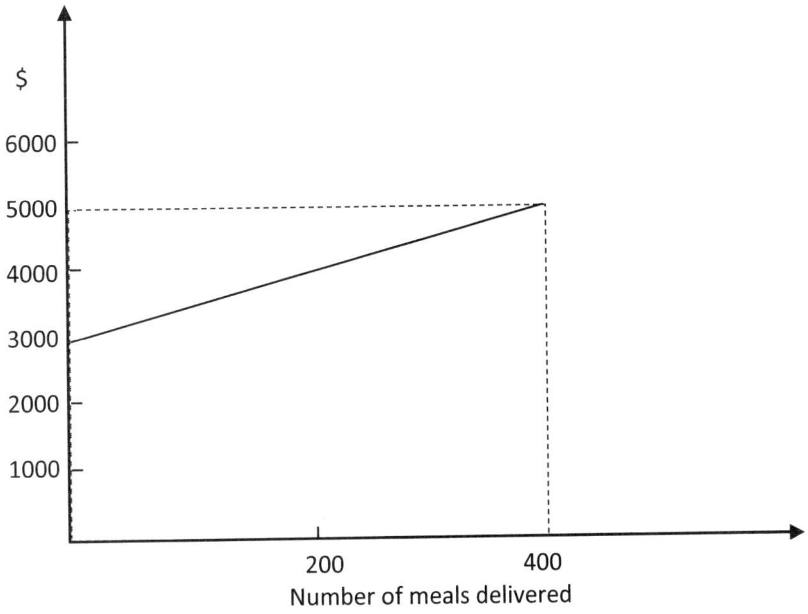

Based on the above scatter graph, the total fixed cost and variable cost per unit would be:

	Total fixed cost	**Variable cost per unit**
A	\$3,000	\$5.00
B	\$3,000	\$10.00
C	\$5,000	\$5.00
D	\$5,000	\$10.00

22 A project requires an initial investment of \$450,000. The company uses NPV to appraise projects. The following cash flows have been estimated for the life of the project:

Year	**1**	**2**	**3**	**4**
Cash flow (\$)	120,000	150,000	160,000	120,000

Using a discount rate of 7%, calculate the NPV of the project. \$____________

23 **Select the correct word to complete the following sentences.**

Management/financial accounting is a statutory requirement.

Management/financial accounting is governed by many rules and regulations.

Management/financial accounting can be presented in any format.

24 Which TWO of the following would NOT be included in a cash budget?

- [ ] Depreciation
- [ ] Receipts from credit sales
- [ ] Provisions for doubtful debts
- [ ] Wages and salaries
- [ ] Purchase of non-current asset

25 Select the correct term to complete the sentences regarding costs used in decision making.

Notional costs are relevant/irrelevant.

Committed costs are relevant/irrelevant.

Opportunity costs are relevant/irrelevant.

Future, incremental cash flows are relevant/irrelevant.

26 RST is a furniture manufacturer, specialising in solid wood tables.

Consider the following list of costs which RST incurs.

Categorise each cost by nature and element.

	Direct/ Indirect	**Labour/ Material Expense**
The wood used in the manufacture of the tables.		
The heating and lighting of the factory		
The factory manager's salary		
The wages of the staff in the assembly department		
The varnish used to coat the completed tables		

27 XYZ is preparing its budgets for the forthcoming year.

The estimated sales for the first four months of the year are as follows:

Month 1	6,000 units
Month 2	7,000 units
Month 3	5,500 units
Month 4	6,000 units

40% of each month's sales units are to be produced in the month of sale and the balance is to be produced in the previous month.

Calculate the production budget for Month 1. ____________ units.

28 The following extract is taken from the overhead budget of XYZ:

Budgeted activity	50%	75%
Budgeted overhead	$100,000	$112,500

The overhead budget for an activity level of 80% would be:

A $115,000

B $120,000

C $150,000

D $160,000

29 XYZ and LMN are two manufacturing companies. In XYZ the finance team are spread throughout the company, with each working closely with a particular business area. In LMN all the finance staff work together in one team and the team supports the whole company.

Select the correct term to complete the sentences below regarding the way XYZ and LMN have structured their finance functions.

- XYZ has positioned finance as dedicated business partners/a shared services centre/ business process outsourcing.
- LMN has positioned finance as dedicated business partners/a shared services centre/ business process outsourcing.

30 A baker produces four flavours of their best-selling cupcake (chocolate, vanilla, lemon and strawberry) in equal quantities. For quality checking purposes, one cake is selected from each batch of 100 cakes produced.

Calculate the probability that the cake selected is chocolate flavoured? ____________%

31 The balanced scorecard has four perspectives:

- Financial
- Customer
- Learning and growth
- Internal business processes

The following is a list of goals which a manufacturing company has set for the next period.

Drag the perspectives against the appropriate goal.

- To increase the percentage of staff time spent on training
- To increase net profit margin
- To reduce the number of customer complaints
- To reduce the amount of loss in the production process

32 Consider the following investment appraisal techniques.

- NPV
- IRR
- Payback

Match the techniques with the following features by ticking the boxes.

Feature	NPV	IRR	Payback
Takes account of the time value of money			
Considers how quickly the project will pay back the initial investment			
Uses cash flows			
It is an absolute measure			

33 **A flexible budget is**

A A budget of variable production costs only

B A budget which is updated with actual costs and revenues as they occur during the budget period

C A budget which shows the costs and revenues at different levels of activity

D A budget which is prepared for a period of six months and reviewed monthly. Following such a review, a further one month's budget is prepared.

34

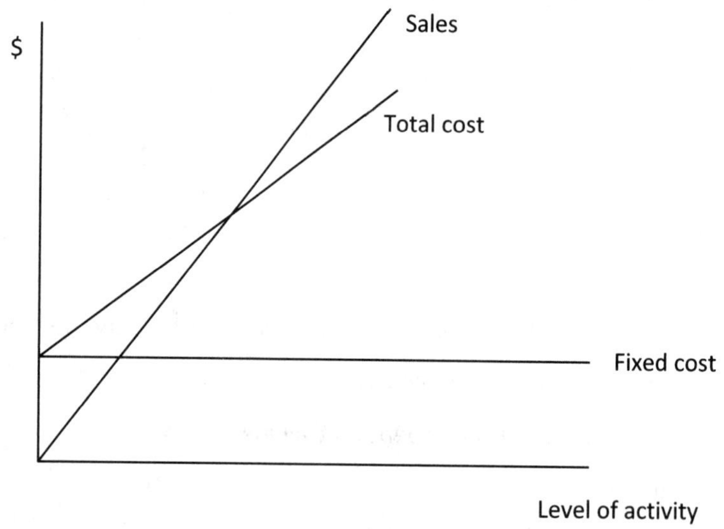

This graph is known as a

A semi-variable cost chart

B conventional breakeven chart

C contribution breakeven chart

D profit volume chart

35 **Select the correct term to complete the sentences regarding performance measures.**

A An example of a financial/non-financial performance measure is gross margin %.

B One problem of using financial/ non- financial performance measures alone is that it can lead to a short-term focus.

C Financial/non-financial performance measures tend to focus on productivity and quality.

D An example of a financial/non-financial performance measure is delivery time.

36 Not-for-profit organisations often use the 3E concept to measure performance.

The three Es are:

- Efficiency
- Economy
- Effectiveness

A hospital has set the following performance goals:

- To maximise the bed occupancy rate
- To minimise patient waiting times
- To reduce the total staff cost while maintaining the level of service.

Match the goals to whether they relate to efficiency, effectiveness or economy.

37 The labour requirement for a special contract is 250 skilled labour hours (paid $10 per hour) and 750 semi-skilled labour hours (paid $8 per hour).

At present skilled labour is in short supply, and all such labour used on this contract will be at the expense of other work which generates $12 contribution per hour (after charging labour costs). There is currently a surplus of 1,200 semi-skilled labour hours, but the company currently has a policy of no redundancies.

The relevant cost of labour for the special contract is:

A $3,000

B $5,500

C $8,500

D $9,000

38 **Which TWO of the following are prime costs?**

☐	Direct materials
☐	Indirect labour
☐	Variable overheads
☐	Indirect expenses
☐	Direct labour

The next two questions are based on the following data.

PQR has prepared the following standard cost information for one unit of product X:

Direct materials	2 kg at $13/per kg	$26.00
Direct labour	3.3 hours at $14/per hour	$46.20

Actual results for the period were recorded as follows:

Production	12,000 units
Materials – 26,400 kg	$336,600
Labour – 40,200 hours	$570,840

All of the materials were purchased and used during the period.

39 The direct material price and usage variances are:

	Material price	**Material usage**
A	$6,600 (F)	$31,200 (A)
B	$6,600 (F)	$31,200 (F)
C	$31,200 (F)	$6,600 (A)
D	$31,200 (A)	$6,600 (A)

40 The direct labour rate and efficiency variances are:

	Labour rate	**Labour efficiency**
A	$8,040 (A)	$8,400 (A)
B	$8,040 (A)	$8,400 (F)
C	$8,040 (F)	$8,400 (A)
D	$8,040 (F)	$8,400 (F)

41 A company has compiled data on the number of items purchased by a customer in his last 7 orders:

10, 22, 3, 6, 17, 14, 19

Which TWO of the following statements are correct?

- ☐ The arithmetic mean is 13
- ☐ The median is 6
- ☐ The arithmetic mean is 15
- ☐ The median is 14
- ☐ The arithmetic mean value is higher than the median value

42 **Which of the following are objectives of budgeting?**

(i) Resource allocation

(ii) Expansion

(iii) Communication

(iv) Co-ordination

A (i), (ii)

B (i), (ii), (iii)

C (i), (iii), (iv)

D (i), (ii), (iii), (iv)

43 Four products have the same mean weight of 250 grams but their standard deviations are:

Product A	10 grams
Product B	15 grams
Product C	20 grams
Product D	25 grams

Which product has the highest coefficient of variation?

A Product A

B Product B

C Product C

D Product D

44 Data for product Q are as follows.

Direct material cost per unit	$54
Direct labour cost per unit	$87
Direct labour hours per unit	11 hours
Production overhead absorption rate	$7 per direct labour hour
Mark-up for non-production overhead costs	3%

10,000 units of product Q are budgeted to be sold each year. Product Q requires an investment of $220,000 and the target rate of return on investment is 14 % per annum.

Calculate the selling price for one unit of product Q (to the nearest cent). $____________

45 X manufactures a product called the 'ZT'. The budget for next year is:

Annual sales	10,000 units
	$ per unit
Selling price	20
Variable cost	14
Fixed costs	3

If the selling price of the ZT was reduced by 10%, calculate the sales revenue that would be needed to generate the original budgeted profit. $____________

46 Which TWO of the following would contribute towards a favourable sales price variance?

- [ ] The standard sales price per unit was set too high
- [ ] Price competition in the market was not as fierce as expected
- [ ] Sales volume was higher than budgeted and therefore sales revenue was higher than budgeted
- [ ] The standard sales price was set too low
- [ ] Increased availability of substitute products in the market

47 Which TWO of the following statements relating to overheads are correct?

- [ ] Overheads are also known as prime costs
- [ ] Overhead absorption rates are used to charge overhead to products
- [ ] If actual overheads are lower than absorbed overhead there will be an under absorption
- [ ] Overheads are always fixed
- [ ] In marginal costing, fixed overheads are treated as period costs

48 A management consultancy recovers overheads on the basis of chargeable consulting hours. Budgeted overheads were $615,000 and actual consulting hours were 32,150. Overheads were under-recovered by $35,000.

If actual overheads were $694,075, the budgeted overhead absorption rate per hour was $____________

49 JKL has recently employed P, a management accountant, who previously worked for a rival company, RST. P has provided the board of JKL with sensitive information about RST. He has also encouraged the board to appoint PQR as their new main supplier of materials. PQR is a company owned by his wife.

Which TWO fundamental principles have been breached?

A Integrity and professional competence and due care

B Objectivity and professional behaviour

C Confidentiality and Objectivity

D Professional competence and due care and confidentiality

50 A group of workers have a weekly wage which is normally distributed with a mean of $360 per week and a standard deviation of $15.

What is the probability that a worker earns more than $380? (to the nearest %)

A 4%

B 5%

C 7%

D 9%

51 The following pie chart shows the sales from the three divisions of a company.

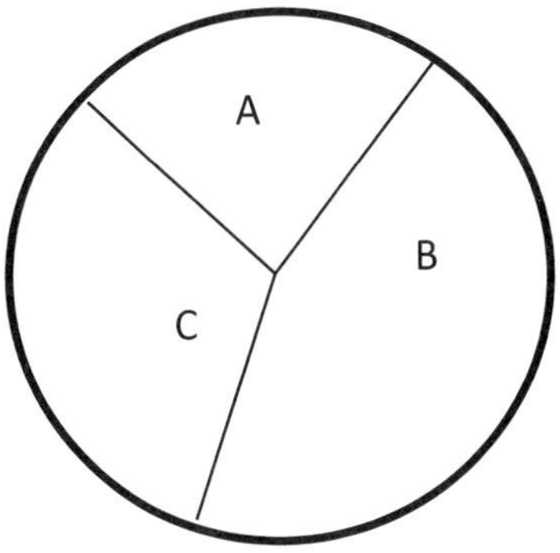

The total sales were $900,000. The angle of the section showing division B's sales is 175° and the angle of the section showing division C's sales is 100°.

Calculate the amount of sales from Division A (to the nearest $). $___________

52 **In a forecasting model based on y = a + bx, the intercept is $234. If the value of y is $491 and x = 20 then b is equal to?**

A 12.25

B 12.85

C 13.35

D 13.95

53 XYZ sells specialist cupcakes to customers to eat on their premises or to take away.

The manager has established that the cost of ingredients is a wholly variable cost in relation to the number of cupcakes sold whereas staff costs are semi-variable and rent costs are fixed.

Select the correct word to complete the sentences to explain what happens, within the relevant range, as the number of cupcakes increases.

- The ingredients cost per cupcake sold will increase/decrease/stay the same.
- The staff cost per cupcake sold will increase/decrease/stay the same.
- The rent cost per cupcake sold will increase/decrease/stay the same.

54 An advertising agency uses a job costing system to calculate the cost of their contracts. Contract A42 was one of several contracts undertaken in the last accounting period. Costs associated with contract A42 are:

Direct materials $5,500

Direct expenses $14,500

Design staff worked 1,020 hours on contract A42, of which 120 hours were overtime. One third of these overtime hours were worked at the request of the client who wanted the contract to be completed quickly. Overtime is paid at a premium of 25% of the basic rate of $24.00 per hour.

Calculate the prime cost of contract A42 to the nearest $. $___________

55

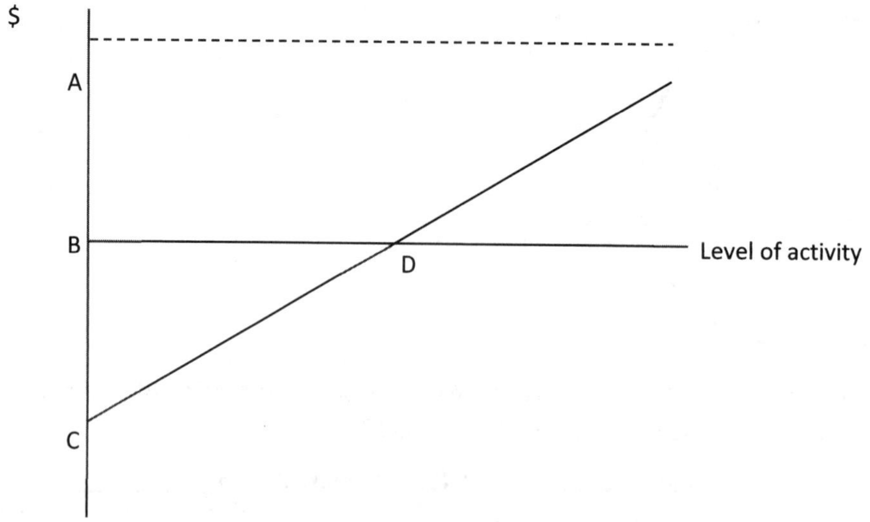

Consider the above PV chart.

Insert the correct word from the following list to explain what is shown by the graph.

- Contribution
- Profit
- Breakeven
- Loss
- Fixed cost
- Variable cost

The difference between A and B	
The difference between B and C	
Point C	
Point D	

56 **Which of the following statements regarding CIMA are correct?**

A On completion of the required examinations a student will become a member of CIMA.

B Students must comply with CIMA's code of ethics from when they become members of CIMA.

C CIMA only supports organisations in the public sector.

D CIMA is the largest professional body of management accountants in the world.

57 JKL produces three products A, B and C which all require skilled labour. This is limited to 6,100 hours per month.

	A	**B**	**C**
Labour hours per unit	1	3	1.5
Contribution per unit	$30	$15	$20
Maximum sales	2,500 units	1,000 units	2,000 units

In order to maximise profits for the month, production quantities of each product should be?

A A 2,500 B 200 C 2,000

B A 2,500 B 1,000 C 2,000

C A 2,500 B 1,000 C 1,000

D A 2,000 B 1,000 C 2,000

58 A newsagent buys daily newspapers each day which have a resale value at the end of the day of zero. Newspaper W is bought for $0.15 each and sold for $0.30 each. The levels of demand per day and their associated probabilities for newspaper W are as follows.

Demand per day	**Probability**
400	0.2
440	0.35
480	0.35
520	0.1

How many copies of newspaper W should the newsagent buy each day?

A 400

B 440

C 480

D 520

59 CDE makes three components (X, Y and Z). The following unit costs have been ascertained:

	X	Y	Z
	Unit cost	**Unit cost**	**Unit cost**
	$	$	$
Variable cost	5.00	16.00	10.00
Fixed cost	4.00	16.60	7.50
Total cost	9.00	32.60	17.50

Another company has offered to supply the components to CDE at the following prices:

Component	Price per unit
	$
X	8.00
Y	14.00
Z	11.00

Which components, if any, should CDE consider buying in from the other company?

A None of the components

B Component X

C Component Y

D Component Z

60 A project requires an initial investment of $190,000. The company has a cost of capital of 10%. The following cash flows have been estimated for the life of the project:

Year	Cash flow
1	$54,000
2	$68,000
3	$87,000
4	$45,000

Which TWO of the following statements are correct? (use 10% and 20% when calculating the IRR)

- ☐ The IRR of the project is approximately 13%
- ☐ The IRR of the project is approximately 17%
- ☐ The IRR is above the cost of capital so the project should be accepted
- ☐ The IRR is below the cost of capital so the project should be accepted
- ☐ Using NPV would suggest that the project should be rejected

Section 4

ANSWERS TO PRACTICE ASSESSMENT QUESTIONS

1 The correct sentences are:

Cost A is a **fixed** cost.

Cost B is a **variable** cost.

Cost C is a **semi-variable** cost.

Cost D is a **variable** cost.

Cost A is unchanged over the two activity levels which suggest that it is a fixed cost.

Cost B has the same unit cost at both levels ($700 ÷ 200 = $3.50 and $875 ÷ 250 = $3.50) which makes it a variable cost.

Cost C has a unit cost of (2,400 ÷ 200) = $12 for 200 units and ($2,500 ÷ 250) = $10 for 250 units which suggests it is a semi-variable cost. Using the high-low method, you can calculate that this is a semi-variable cost with a fixed element of $2,000 and a variable element of $2 per unit.

Cost D has the same unit cost at both levels ($1,360 ÷ 200 = $6.80 and $1,700 ÷ 250 = $6.80) which makes it a variable cost.

2

✓	Complete
	Concise
✓	Understandable
	Regular
	Responsible
✓	Timely
✓	Accurate
	Effective

3 The present value of the cash flows from the perpetuity is **$766,000**

This is simply a standard perpetuity with one additional payment at T_0. The perpetuity factor = 1 ÷ 0.045 = 22.222

Add 1 as the payments start at once, so the perpetuity factor = 22.222 + 1 = 23.222

Present value = $33,000 × 23.222 = $766,326

4 **B**

Total number of failures = 500 + 200 = 700

Total number of candidates = 1,000 + 500 = 1,500

So the probability of a chosen candidate having failed = 700 in 1,500, or 0.47.

This could also be calculated as:

P (failed) = 1 – P (passed) = 1 – (800/1,500) = 0.47 or 47%

5 **C**

The probability of being located in Europe and that they failed

= probability of location in Europe × probability of a fail

= (1,000 ÷1,500) × (500 ÷ 1,000) = 0.33 or 33%

6 **A**

The principal budget factor is the factor which limits the activities of the organisation at is often the starting point in budget preparation.

7 **C**

	$
Marginal costing profit	850,500
Change in inventory × OAR	
(34,000 – 31,000) × OAR	105,000
Absorption costing profit	955,500

OAR = $105,000 ÷ 3,000 = $35 per unit

Level of activity = $1,837,500 ÷ £35 = **52,500 units**

8 **D**

The $200,000 entry represents the transfer to the finished goods account.

9 **D**

Rent Department A = (2,000 ÷ 5,000) × $40,000 = $16,000

Rent Department B = (2,500 ÷ 5,000) × $40,000 = $20,000

So Department A + Department B = $16,000 + $20,000 = $36,000

10

	Debit	**Credit**	**No entry in this account**
Production overhead account		✓	
Work in progress account			✓
Statement of profit or loss	✓		

11 The amount of overhead to be added to job CC20 for the period is **$73,800.**

Overhead absorption will be based on labour cost.

Total labour cost = $14,500 + $3,500 + $24,600 = $42,600

Overhead absorption rate = $127,800 ÷ $42,600 = $3 per $ of labour cost

Job CC20 will pick up ($3 × $24,600) = $73,800

12 The cost per tonne-mile is **$2.80**

Total tonne-miles = (5,000 × 250) = 1,250,000

Cost per tonne-mile = $3,500,000 ÷ 1,250,000 = $2.80

13 C

Product A expected value

= (0.4 × $600) + (0.6 × $100) = $240 + $60 = $300

Product B expected value

= (0.6 × $400) + (0.4 × –$50) = $240 – $20 = $220

Product A has a higher expected value so select A

14 The completed table is shown below:

	A	**B**	**C**
Sales revenue	✓		✓
Staff costs	✓	✓	✓
Capital investment			✓
Administration expenses	✓	✓	✓

Cost centre managers are responsible for managing costs. Profit centre managers are responsible for costs and revenues and investment centre managers are responsible for costs, revenues and capital invested.

15 A

Year	Cash flow $000	Cumulative cash flow $000
0	(1,200)	(1,200)
1	240	(960)
2	265	(695)
3	240	(455)
4	660	205
5	290	495

Payback is achieved between years 3 and 4.

Payback is 3 years plus (455/660 × 12) months = 3 years 9 months (remember to round up when using payback).

This is less than the target payback period of 4 years therefore the investment should be undertaken.

16 The total overhead for the machining department is **$2,850,000**

Let Stores = S and Maintenance = M

M = 800,000 + 0.4S (1)

S = 250,000 + 0.25M (2)

Substitute (1) in (2):

S = 250,000 + 0.25 (800,000 + 0.4S)

S = 250,000 + 200,000 + 0.1S

0.9S = 450,000

S = 500,000

Substituting this into equation (1)

M = 800,000 + 0.4(500,000) = 1,000,000

Total overheads for Machining department:

= 2,250,000 + (30% × 500,000) + (45% × 1,000,000) = $2,850,000

17

✓	The principles should be used my management accountants as a guide to best practice.
✓	One of the key aims of the principles is to encourage integrated thinking within organisations.
	The principles are a statutory requirement for all members of CIMA.
	The four principles are influence, trust, reliability and value
	Two of the principles are integrity and objectivity

The principles are not a statutory requirement, but are designed as a guide to best practice within management accounting.

The four principles are influence, trust, relevance and value.

Objectivity and integrity are two of the fundamental principles of the CIMA code of ethics.

18 A

The actual contribution earned by RST last month was

= (32,000 – 800 – 880 + 822 + 129 + 89) = $31,360.

19 The complete sentences are:

Total **fixed** cost, within a relevant range, is not affected by changes in activity levels.

Fixed cost per unit **reduces** as the activity level increases.

Total variable cost **increases** as the activity level increases.

On a graph showing activity level on the x axis and cost on the y axis, **variable** cost per unit would be shown as a horizontal line.

20 The present value of the cash flows from the annuity is **$30,885**

This is a standard 14-year annuity with one additional payment at T_0.

The 6% 14-year annuity factor is 9.295.

Add 1 as the payments start at once, so the annuity factor = (9.295 + 1) = 10.295

Present value = $3,000 × 10.295 = $30,885

21 A

The total fixed cost is $3,000 (where the line crosses the y axis)

Variable cost per meal = ($5,000 – $3,000) ÷ (400 – 0) = $5

22 This project has a **positive NPV of $15,270.**

Year	Cash flow ($)	Discount factor (7%)	Present value ($)
0	(450,000)	1	(450,000)
1	120,000	0.935	112,200
2	150,000	0.873	130,950
3	160,000	0.816	130,560
4	120,000	0.763	91,560
		NPV =	15,270

23 The complete sentences are:

Financial accounting is a statutory requirement.

Financial accounting is governed by many rules and regulations.

Management accounting can be presented in any format.

24

✓	Depreciation
	Receipts from credit sales
✓	Provisions for doubtful debts
	Wages and salaries
	Purchase of non-current asset

Depreciation and provision for doubtful debts are not cash flows so would not be included in the cash budget.

25 The complete sentences are:

Notional costs are **irrelevant.**

Committed costs are **irrelevant.**

Opportunity costs are **relevant.**

Future, incremental cash flows are **relevant.**

26 The correct categorisation is:

	Direct/ Indirect	**Labour/ Material Expense**
The wood used in the manufacture of the tables.	**Direct**	**Material**
The heating and lighting of the factory	**Indirect**	**Expense**
The factory manager's salary	**Indirect**	**Labour**
The wages of the staff in the assembly department	**Direct**	**Labour**
The varnish used to coat the completed tables	**Indirect**	**Material**

27 The production budget for month 1 will be **6,600 units.**

	Month 1 Units	**Month 2 Units**
Sales	6,000	7,000
Production:		
40% in the month	2,400	2,800
60% in the previous month	4,200	3,300
Production	6,600	6,100

28 A

Using the high/low method:

		$	
High	75%	112,500	
Low	50%	100,000	
Change	25%	12,500	– variable cost of 25%
	1%	500	– variable cost of 1%

	$
Using 75% activity:	
Total overhead	112,500
Variable cost element (75 × $500)	37,500
Fixed cost element	75,000
Total overhead for 80% activity:	
Variable cost element (80 × $500)	40,000
Fixed cost element	75,000
Total overhead	115,000

29 The correct sentences are:

XYZ has positioned finance as **dedicated business partners.**

LMN has positioned finance as a **shared services centre.**

30 The probability that the cake selected is chocolate flavoured is **25%.**

In each batch of 100, 25 of the cakes will be chocolate flavoured.

The probability of selecting a chocolate cake will be 25 in 100 = 0.25 or 25%.

31 The correct matching is:

- To increase the percentage of staff time spent on training – **Learning and growth**
- To increase net profit margin – **Financial**
- To reduce the number of customer complaints – **Customer**
- To reduce the amount of loss in the production process – **Internal business processes**

32 The correct matching is:

Feature	**NPV**	**IRR**	**Payback**
Takes account of the time value of money	✓	✓	
Considers how quickly the project will pay back the initial investment			✓
Uses cash flows	✓	✓	✓
It is an absolute measure	✓		

33 **C**

A flexible budget is one which shows the costs and revenues at different levels of activity.

34 **B**

The graph is known as a conventional breakeven chart which shows total sales revenue and total costs. The breakeven point is shown at the point at which the two lines intersect.

35 The completed sentences are:

A An example of a **financial** performance measure is gross margin %.

B One problem of using **financial** performance measures alone is that it can lead to a short-term focus.

C **Non-financial** performance measures tend to focus on productivity and quality.

D An example of a **non-financial** performance measure is delivery time.

36 The correct matching is:

- To maximise the bed occupancy rate – **efficiency**
- To minimise patient waiting times – **effectiveness**
- To reduce the total staff cost while maintaining the level of service – **economy**

37 **B**

The relevant cost of labour is $5,500

		$
Skilled labour: basic pay	(250 × $10)	2,500
Skilled labour: contribution forgone	(250 × $12)	3,000
Unskilled labour – will be paid anyway		0
		5,500

Contribution is measured after deducting the basic labour cost, so the relevant cost of the scarce skilled labour is the basic pay plus the contribution obtainable from doing the other work.

38

✓	Direct materials
	Indirect labour
	Variable overheads
	Indirect expenses
✓	Direct labour

Prime costs consist of direct materials, direct labour and direct expenses.

39 A

	$
26,400kg should have cost (× $13)	343,200
But did cost	336,600
Materials price variance	$6,600 F
12,000 units should have used (× 2kg)	24,000 kg
But did use	26,400 kg
Variance in kg	2,400 A
× standard price	× $13
Materials usage variance	$31,200 A

40 A

	$
40,200 hours should cost (× $14)	562,800
But did cost	570,840
Labour rate variance	$8,040 A
12,000 units should have taken (× 3.3 hrs)	39,600
But did take	40,200
Variance in hours	600 A
× standard rate	× $14
Labour efficiency variance	$8,400 A

41

✓	The arithmetic mean is 13
	The median is 6
	The arithmetic mean is 15
✓	The median is 14
	The arithmetic mean value is higher than the median value

The median is the value of the middle item. So if the numbers are put in order:

3, 6, 10, 14, 17, 19, 22

The median is 14.

The arithmetic mean = (3 + 6 + 10 + 14 + 17 + 19 + 22) ÷ 7 = 13

42 C

Resource allocation, communication and co-ordination are all objectives of budgeting. Expansion is not generally an objective of budgeting.

43 D

Coefficient of variation = standard deviation ÷ Mean

Product A (10 ÷ 250) × 100 = 4%

Product B (15 ÷ 250) × 100 = 6%

Product C (20 ÷ 250) × 100 = 8%

Product D (25 ÷ 250) × 100 = 10%

So Product D has the highest coefficient of variation.

44 The selling price for one unit of product Q, to the nearest cent, is **$227.62**

	$ per unit
Direct material cost	54.00
Direct labour cost	87.00
Total direct cost	141.00
Production overhead absorbed (11 hours × $7)	77.00
Total production cost	218.00
Mark-up for non-production costs (3% × $218.00)	6.54
Full cost	224.54
Profit (see working)	3.08
Selling price	227.62

Working:

Target return on investment in product Q = $220,000 × 14% = $30,800

Target return per unit of product Q = $30,800/10,000 units = $3.08.

45 The sales revenue that would be needed to generate the original budgeted profit would be **$270,000.**

Fixed costs are not relevant because they will remain unaltered.

Original budgeted contribution = 10,000 units × $(20 – 14) = $60,000

Revised selling price = $20 – 10% = $18

Revised contribution per unit = $(18 – 14) = $4

Required number of units to achieve same contribution = $60,000/$4 = 15,000 units

Required sales revenue: 15,000 units × $18 revised price = $270,000

46

	The standard sales price per unit was set too high
✓	Price competition in the market was not as fierce as expected
	Sales volume was higher than budgeted and therefore sales revenue was higher than budgeted
✓	The standard sales price was set too low
	Increased availability of substitute products in the market

A and E would result in an adverse variance.

Reason C would not necessarily result in any sales price variance because all the units could have been sold at standard price.

47

	Overheads are also known as prime costs
✓	Overhead absorption rates are used to charge overhead to products
	If actual overheads are lower than absorbed overhead there will be an under absorption
	Overheads are always fixed
✓	In marginal costing, fixed overheads are treated as period costs

Overheads are also known as indirect costs; prime costs are direct costs. If actual overheads are lower than absorbed overheads this will result in an over absorption. Overheads can be fixed or variable.

48 The budgeted overhead absorption rate per hour was **$20.50**.

	$
Actual overhead	694,075
Under-recovered overhead	35,000
Absorbed overhead	659,075

Actual consulting hours: 32,150

Absorption rate = $659,075 ÷ 32,150 hours = $20.50 per hour.

49 **C**

Confidentiality means not disclosing information unless you have permission or a legal duty to do so. In this case the accountant has disclosed sensitive information about his previous employer without permission.

Objectivity means acting without bias or conflict of interest. Encouraging the board to select his wife's company as supplier would breach this principle.

50 **D**

$$Z = \frac{X - \mu}{\sigma}$$

Z = (380 – 360) ÷ 15 = 1.33

From normal distribution table:

Z = 0.4082

So probability > Z = 0.5 – 0.4082

= 0.0918

= 9.2%

51 The sales from division A are **$212,500**

There are 360° in a circle, so if cost B and C represent (175 + 100) = 275° then A must represent (360 – 275) = 85°. Therefore the sales from Division A is $\frac{85}{360}$ × $900,000 = $212,500

52 **B**

y = a + bx

491 = 234 + 20b

20b = 257

b = 12.85

53 The correct sentences are:

- the ingredients cost per cupcake sold will **stay the same**.
- the staff cost per cupcake sold will **decrease**.
- the rent cost per cupcake sold will **decrease**.

54 The prime cost of contract A42 is **$44,720.**

	$
Direct materials	5,500
Direct expenses	14,500
Basic staff hours (1,020 hrs × $24)	24,480
Overtime premium *(40 hrs × $6)	240
	44,720

* One third of overtime hours were at the request of the customer. These 40 hours will be treated as direct costs. The overtime rate = (25% × $24) = $6.

55 The graph shows the following:

The difference between A and B	**Profit**
The difference between B and C	**Loss**
Point C	**Fixed cost**
Point D	**Breakeven**

56 **D**

To become a member of CIMA, students not only have to complete the required CGMA examinations, they must also demonstrate their experience by completing their professional experience records.

Both members and students must comply with CIMA's code of ethics at all times.

CIMA supports organisations in both the public and the private sector.

57 **A**

	A	**B**	**C**
Contribution	$30	$15	$20
Labour hours	1	3	1.5
Contribution per labour hour	30	5	13.3
Rank	1	3	2

	Units	**Hours**
Product A	2,500 (2,500 × 1)	2,500
Product C	2,000 (2,000 × 1.5)	3,000
Product B	200 (200 ×3)	600
		6,100

58 B

Purchase 400/Sell 400, 440, 480, 520: Profit = (400 × \$30) – (400 × \$15) = \$60.

Purchase 440/Sell 400: Profit = (400 × \$30) – (440 × \$15) = \$54.

Purchase 440/Sell 440, 480, 520: Profit = (440 × \$30) – (440 × \$15) = \$66.

Purchase 480/Sell 400: Profit = (400 × \$30) – (480 × \$15) = \$48.

Purchase 480/Sell 440: Profit = (440 × \$30) – (480 × \$15) = \$60.

Purchase 480/Sell 480, 520: Profit = (480 × \$30) – (480 × \$15) = \$72.

Purchase 520/Sell 400: Profit = (400 × \$30) – (520 × \$15) = \$42.

Purchase 520/Sell 440: Profit = (440 × \$30) – (520 × \$15) = \$54.

Purchase 520/Sell 480: Profit = (480 × \$30) – (520 × \$15) = \$66.

Purchase 520/Sell 520: Profit = (520 × \$30) – (520 × \$15) = \$78.

So a payoff table would look like:

Demand			**Purchased per day**		
	Prob	400	440	480	520
400	0.2	\$60	\$54	\$48	\$42
440	0.35	\$60	\$66	\$60	\$54
480	0.35	\$60	\$66	\$72	\$66
520	0.1	\$60	\$66	\$72	\$78

To calculate the expected value:

Buy 400: \$60

Buy 440: (0.2 × 54) + (0.8 × 66) = 63.6

Buy 480: (0.2 × 48) + (0.35 × 60) + (0.45 × 72) = 63

Buy 520: (0.2 × 42) + (0.35 × 54) + (0.35 × 66) + (0.1 × 78) = 58.2

Highest expected value 440 = \$63.60.

59 C

	X	**Y**	**Z**
	\$	\$	\$
Variable cost of manufacture	5	16	10
Cost of external purchase	8	14	11
Saving/(cost) of external purchase	(3)	2	(1)

On the assumption that fixed overhead costs would be unaffected by a decision to switch to external purchasing, CDE should consider buying only component Y externally.

60

✓	The IRR of the project is approximately 13%
	The IRR of the project is approximately 17%
✓	The IRR is above the cost of capital so the project should be accepted
	The IRR is below the cost of capital so the project should be accepted
	Using NPV would suggest that the project should be rejected

			Discount factor 10%		**Discount factor 20%**	
Year		Cash flow $	DF (10%)	PV $	DF (20%)	PV $
0		(190,000)	1	(190,000)	1	(190,000)
1		54,000	0.909	49,086	0.833	44,982
2		68,000	0.826	56,168	0.694	47,192
3		87,000	0.751	65,337	0.579	50,373
4		45,000	0.683	30,735	0.482	21,690
			NPV =	**11,326**	**NPV =**	**(25,763)**

The NPV has changed by $37,089

The discount rate has changed by 10%

Therefore the NPV changes $3,709.9 for every 1% change in the discount rate ($37,089 / 10)

The IRR will be 10% + ($11,326 / $3,709.9) = 10 + 0.305

IRR = 13.05%

The IRR could also have been estimated using the formula or graphical method.

The IRR is more than the cost of capital; therefore the project should be accepted. Using a discount rate of 10%, the NPV is positive, therefore the project should be accepted.

How to access your online resources

Kaplan Financial students will have a MyKaplan account and these extra resources will be available to you online. You do not need to register again, as this process was completed when you enrolled. If you are having problems accessing online materials, please ask your course administrator.

If you are not studying with Kaplan and did not purchase your book via a Kaplan website, to unlock your extra online resources please go to **www.mykaplan.co.uk/add-online-resources** (even if you have set up an account and registered books previously). You will then need to enter the ISBN number (on the title page and back cover) and the unique pass key number contained in the scratch panel below to gain access.

You will also be required to enter additional information during this process to set up or confirm your account details.

If you purchased through the Kaplan Publishing website you will automatically receive an e-mail invitation to register your details and gain access to your content. If you do not receive the e-mail or book content, please contact Kaplan Publishing.

This code can only be used once for the registration of this book online. This registration and your online content will expire when the examinations covered by this book have taken place. Please allow one hour from the time you submit your book details for us to process your request.

Please scratch the film to access your unique code.

Please be aware that this code is case-sensitive and you will need to include the dashes within the passcode, but not when entering the ISBN.

KAPLAN PUBLISHING